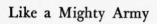

Like a Mighty Army

Halford E. Luccock

Like a Mighty Army

SELECTED LETTERS OF SIMEON STYLITES

New York

OXFORD UNIVERSITY PRESS

1954

Foreword

I know very little about the original Simeon Stylites, except that he was the forerunner of all columnists. According to the *Encyclopedia Britannica* he seems to have had a compulsive affinity for columns, roosting first on top of one only six feet tall, but gradually gaining confidence until he soared thirty feet aloft. From that eminence, tradition affirms, he virtually ruled Syria for thirty years of the turbulent fifth century. Ensconced above the preoccupations of the common herd, in a vantage spot from which he could view far horizons as well as the daily turmoil at his feet, he won a reputation through all Asia Minor for unsurpassed wisdom sustained by a nearly incredible piety.

I make no claims about the extent to which Halford E. Luccock, who writes the weekly Simeon Stylites column in *The Christian Century,* lives up to the latter aspect of that tradition. Nor need I claim that this

modern Simeon Stylites is wise. To do so would be like
claiming that the sun is dazzling. But I can testify,
on the evidence of an editor's mail, that a good many
people scattered over every continent would sooner
go without all the rest of their intellectual diet than
be deprived of the stimulus they regularly obtain from
the Stylites letters. Indeed, they have become a constant antidote for any budding editorial pride, for
I seldom discuss the *Century* with a reader without
hearing, "Well, there's at least one feature I never
miss — Simeon Stylites."

When it was announced that publication of a collection of the Simeon Stylites letters was under con-
sideration, suggestions about its contents poured in.
One that I particularly liked came from a Japanese
who said that he regularly relies on Simeon to provide the punch in his sermons. It should be interesting to hear Simeon in Japanese idiom! If all the nom-
inations had been included — and they all deserved
inclusion — this book would have swollen to unman-
ageable proportions. What is printed here, therefore,
is not presented as "the best" of Simeon. But it is representative. And it will make plain the reason why I
account it such good fortune to have the first chance,
week after week, to read the most sparkling columnar
essays now being contributed to the American press.

For the benefit of *The Christian Century,* I hope
that Halford Luccock stays as long in possession of his
column as the Syrian pillar-sitter did of his.

Paul Hutchinson.

Contents

'Like a Mighty Army — ,' 3

The Man from Porlock, 5

He Rang the Bell, 8

The Wife of Sisyphus, 11

Reading from Left to Right, 13

A Partridge in a Pear Tree, 16

Wise Men from the West, 18

A Squeeze of the Lemon, 21

The Blood of the Martyrs, 23

In Absentia, 25

'What Have You Been Doing, Then?' 28

Cadenza, 30

'I Played Their Accompaniment,' 33

Advertising Witchcraft, 35

Irregular, 37

How To Be a Bad Parent, 40

Somebody Must Sell Suspension Bridges, 42

Heresy, 44

The Man Who Caught Up with Himself, 47

Calamity by Flood, 49

The Devils Were White, 51

Enter the Crocus! 53

One Bang, 55

Pentagon, 57

Do-It-Yourself, 60

A Show of Hands, 62

Permission To Shriek, 64

Six Impossible Things before Breakfast, 67

Western Union Theology, 69

A Speech for Any Occasion, 71

His Bite Is Worse than His Bark, 74

The Art of Coming In, 76

The Art of Doing Nothing, 79

The Temperance Society, 81

The Voice of Angels, 83

If the Founders Came Back, 85

Indianapolis! 88

Picking Up Your Cap, 90

Letter to 10,000 Wives, 92

Total Recall, 94

Thirty Pieces of Silver, 97

Bluebeard — American Version, 99

Is There a Doctor in the House? 101

Anoint the Elbows, 103

Apparition at a Board Meeting, 106

Taking Off the Scum, 108

'By the Dawn's Early Light,' 110

'Klunk!' 113

Delilah on the Hearth, 115

'Remain Explosively,' 118

Too Young or Too Old, 120

The Wayward Postman, 123

Wait for the Verb! 125

Good Friday — and a Toothache, 128

'You Must Relax,' 130

The Bull Pen, 132

The Pulpit Committee, 134

Men of Distinction, 137

'He Simply Got Up and Left,' 139

'Teenie-Weenie,' 141

Goops, 143

Paging Mr. Thoreau, 146

The Fifth Freedom, 149

Homage to Button Gwinnett, 152

The *Ding an Sich*, 154

No Boswell, Please! 156

'Late Bloomers,' 159

'Ministers of Grace,' 161

Knowing the Right People, 164

'Hi, Brother!' 166

'Whatever Is Worth Doing . . .' 169

Footnotes, 172

Take a Letter to Yourself, 175

Too Many Shrines, 177

The Cultivation of Vanity, 180

Like a Mighty Army

'Like a Mighty Army —'

EDITOR, THE CHRISTIAN CENTURY:

Sir: I met the pastor of St. John's-by-the-Gas-Station last Monday. He was all lit up — not alcoholically but emotionally. I said, "You must have been pretty good yesterday."

"Better than that," he replied. "I had a guest artist take over. And he took everybody over."

"How come?" I asked.

"It was Layman's Sunday. Usually that Sunday brings joy, like a visit to the dentist. A good thing, but better to look back on than forward to. This year I slipped one over on them. You know Jimmy Mitchell, just back from two years in the army in Korea? I figured he would give Layman's Sunday a shot in the arm, but I didn't reckon on him blowing the place up. He refused at first. Then, with a funny light in his eye, he said he would speak if I had the congrega-

3

tion sing 'Onward, Christian Soldiers' just before he
began. So I had them give forth with song, and then
Jimmy let loose. He didn't waste any time in shadow-
boxing. He waded right in. This is what he said:

　" 'You have been singing

> *Like a mighty army*
> *Moves the church of God.*

That might have been all right once. The trouble is
now that just about ten million men know exactly how
an army moves. And it doesn't move the way a lot of
you folks at St. John's do — or do not. Suppose the
army accepted the lame excuses that many of you people think are good enough to serve as an alibi for not
attending Church Parade.

　" 'Imagine this, if you can. Reveille seven a.m.
Squads on the parade ground. The sergeant barks out,
"Count fours." One! Two! Three! Number Four miss-
ing. Where's Private Smith?

　" ' "Oh," pipes up a chap by the vacant place, "Mr.
Smith was too sleepy to get up this morning. He was
out late last night and needed the sleep. He said to tell
you that he would be with you in spirit."

　" ' "That's fine," says the sergeant. "Remember me
to him."

　" ' "Where's Brown?" asks the sergeant.

　" ' "Oh," puts in another chap, "he's out playing
golf. He gets only one day a week for recreation, and
you know how important that is."

　" ' "Sure, sure," is the sergeant's cheerful answer.

"Hope he has a good game. Where's Robinson?"

" ' "Robinson," explains a buddy, "is sorry not to greet you in person. But he is entertaining guests today and of course couldn't come. Besides, he was at drill last week."

" ' "Thank you," says the sergeant, smiling. "Tell him he is welcome any time he is able to drop in."

" 'Honest, now, did any conversation like that ever happen in any army? Don't make me laugh. If any G.I. tried to pull that stuff he would get twenty days in the guardhouse. Yet you hear stuff like that every week in the church, and said with a straight face, too.

" 'Like a mighty army! Why, if St. John's really moved like a mighty army, a lot of you folks would be court-martialed!'

"That was the general drift," said the pastor gleefully.

"Too bad the stay-aways didn't hear it," I remarked.

"Don't worry. I have it on a tape recorder, and I am going to spring it on them next Easter, instead of the Second Lesson."

Forward March!   SIMEON STYLITES.

The Man from Porlock

Sir: Probably the most famous interruption in all literature was that of the unnamed person who knocked on Coleridge's door when the poet was in full flight composing "Kubla Khan." The learned critics have speculated on what might have been the lines that were to follow. Living on a lower level, I have always wondered who the man was and what he wanted. He goes down in history without a name, just the Man from Porlock.

Picture the scene. Coleridge is casting his magic spell, weaving a circle thrice about someone with flashing eyes and floating hair. But here in Coleridge's own words is what happened:

> The author continued for about three hours in a profound sleep. On awakening he appeared to himself to have a distinct recollection of the whole, and taking his pen, ink and paper, instantly and eagerly wrote down the lines that are here preserved. At this instant he was unfortunately called out by a person on business from Porlock, and detained by him for above an hour, and on his return to the room, found, to his no small surprise and mortification, that . . . with the exception of some eight or ten scattered lines and images, all the rest had passed away.

So, with the lines,

> *For he on honey-dew hath fed,*
> *And drunk the milk of Paradise,*

"Kubla Khan" takes a final bow.

What did the Man from Porlock want? Was he collecting a bill, or selling life insurance or tickets to a raffle? Was he a neighbor who dropped in to give his views on the Napoleonic wars? Did he ever know what he interrupted?

He is a fascinating mystery. But he is no mystery to any parish parson. To the parson, the world seems populated chiefly by Men from Porlock, with an uncanny gift for dropping in just when, at last, the engine in the head seems to have caught hold, tentatively, after much frantic stepping on the self-starter. On one day this Man from Porlock is the representative of the *Atomic Book of Facts,* $4.95 in the cloth binding, no home complete without one. An hour later he is the secretary of the World Improvement Association; will the pastor be a director? The next day he is Mr. Crackenfuss, who has called to disclose, *seriatim* and *in extenso,* what was wrong with last Sunday's sermon. The next day he is the district secretary of the Next Crusade, with the quota for the church dexterously concealed on his person. Porlock forever!

And the *Woman* from Porlock! O boy — or, more accurately, O girl! At ten o'clock she is the mother of little Clarence, who must have a different Sunday school teacher, one who understands the child. (He dare not tell her that everyone understands Clarence only too well.) At eleven o'clock she is the chairman of Circle C of the Woman's Society; will he please read a play they would like to give, to see if it is proper? (He fears it is.) The next day she is the president of the Woman's Club, which is arranging its fall meetings; will he give a lecture on "Pansies in World Literature"? Next comes — just when he has caught a distant view of his second point — Mrs. Richardson, to talk over the choir, particularly the soprano, whose voice is getting "raspy" and who, in fact, is not nearly as good as Mrs. Richardson's daughter Grace, who was told by her teacher at the conservatory that she has an "unusual" voice. There will always be a Porlock!

One sweetly solemn thought comes to the pastor, however. What the Man — or Woman — from Porlock is interrupting is probably not a "Kubla Khan."

Yours,

SIMEON STYLITES.

He Rang the Bell

Sir: I am warning you. This is an evangelistic onslaught. So if you don't want to be evangelized, skip it.

One of the forgotten events in American lore which deserve to be recalled frequently is the mad act of Edward Dickinson of Amherst, Massachusetts, the father of Emily Dickinson. He has been so often cast as the heavy villain that I take pleasure in hereby awarding him an Order of Merit with crossed palms. Emily thus records his act:

> We were all startled by a violent fire bell ringing, and thinking of nothing but fire we rushed out into the street to see. A lovely evening sky

colored gorgeously with pink and gold displayed itself to the wondering and admiring people who issued from the houses at Mr. Dickinson's authoritative summons. For father happened to see it first, and rang the fire bell to call attention.

An eminently sound idea — ring the fire bell to get attention to a sunset. And the evangelistic plea is: Oh sinner, there are not enough fire bells sounding. Ring a few. Do some violent attention-calling when you come across an experience that is a lot better show than a three-alarm fire. And if, in these years, we have fewer occasions for enthusiasm running wild, make the most of them.

This applies to sunsets and all such. All over the country this gorgeous autumn there are sights of foliage which demand that we run, not walk, to the nearest firehouse and start the clapper going in the bell. I know that the alarm that Edna St. Vincent Millay sent out,

Oh world, I cannot hold thee close enough,

was a poem in honor of spring. But autumn deserves a fire bell even more. Bliss Carman was a good fire laddie:

> *The scarlet of the maples*
> *Can shake me like a cry*
> *Of bugles going by.*

Too many people are in danger of becoming so intellectualized (real or imaginary) or so spiritualized genuine or imitation) that they cease to live in the physical world with its amazing wonders. Bliss Perry wrote of the Puritans that they often had to hold on hard to the huckleberry bushes to keep from being translated. We all ought to have huckleberry bushes to hold on to — quite literally, for the lowly huckleberry bush is a joy forever. Suppose the birds do get all the berries, you still have flowers that bloom in the spring and lovely leaves that stick around all year and turn a deep red in the fall.

Some people are occasions for dashing into the nearest firehouse and banging the bell. To paraphrase Stevenson, a genuinely great person is a more exciting thing to meet than a hundred-dollar bill. Here I clang the bell for some great persons I recently met in print. There is the Christian family who walk in glory through the pages of that memorable book, Ann Frank's *Diary of a Young Girl* — the family in Belgium who during the last war took into their home a family of Jews and kept them for a year, when every hour meant the risk of life and dividing their slender food ration. Think of that demonstration of what Christian love means! Another experience that calls for bell ringing is the recent book *Strengthened with Might,* by Harold Wilke, which tells of triumphing over an almost insuperable handicap — being born without arms. There *are* flashes struck from midnights!

And here's one more. When the bitterness of today's world gets you down, find your way to the edges of one of these small groups of students — they are springing up all over the country — who are saying they mean to live for causes and not cash, for brotherhood proclaimed in life, not in word. Here's a light in our darkness.

Fire! Fire!

Yours,

SIMEON STYLITES.

The Wife of Sisyphus

Sir: One figure of Greek mythology who has always greatly interested me and drawn my sympathy is Merope, the wife of Sisyphus. Sisyphus was the unlucky chap who, you remember, in the world of the shades, had to roll a huge stone up the hill till it reached the top, only to have it always roll down again to the bottom; an endless, unvarying heartbreaking job.

I have often wondered just what technique his wife found most effective. Did she say every time the stone rolled down, "Tough break, old top. But up and at 'em again"? The poor old boy might get pretty tired of that. Or did she take another tack: "For Jupiter's sake, forget that silly old stone. Let it alone. You can't win"? The trouble with that would be that rolling up the stone was his job and he couldn't resign.

One modern Sisyphus is the pastor of a church.

Every week, with many a huff and puff, he rolls the big stone up to the top on Sunday morning. Every Sunday night it rolls down to the bottom. Even Sunday noon, standing at the door of the church, he often wonders whether he has said anything at all; all the comments are on the weather. Monday morning he starts the long push again. It is an endless hill through the year. All during Lent he is shoving the stone up to the top of Easter morning. Then, plunk! next morning it is down at the bottom again. No wonder they call the Sunday after Easter Low Sunday. Even at best, the pastor's account of his work is like that of the Australian prizefighter who wired his father after a bout, "Won easily in 84 rounds."

What of Merope, the pastor's wife? How should she deal with these unending ups and downs? Sometimes she tries the role of "constructive critic," thus: "Sisyphus, my dear, why don't you try shoving it up on the bias and then giving a little hitch and twist at the top? That would hold it." Some wives even turn on this helpful criticism on Sunday night. That is plainly against Scripture, for the Good Book says, "A broken reed he shall not break." The pastor is a broken reed on many a Sunday night all right. The ram's-horn resonance has gone from his voice and spirit. And even when the helpful criticism is put off for a day, it is not exactly balm in Gilead.

Strangely enough, the best thing that Merope can do for any Sisyphus is to help him forget, for a while, the big stone and the hill. The "ideal" wife, who appears in all the books on the subject and in the dream of many an innocent student, the well-trained associate who is right in there helping all the time, is often a burden too grievous to be borne. She is likely to say, "Now, dear Sisyphus, we can have a nice long evening working out the curriculum for the intermediate grade." Or, "Now we can plan that party for Circle C." The poor man is likely to fall into profanity.

The wisest Merope is more apt to say, "Well, Sis, that old stone will stay there safely overnight. We don't have to watch it. Let's step out and trip the light fantastic." Of course the original Merope didn't say exactly that, for she had not read John Milton, back in those days. But the Greeks had a word for it, I'm sure.

Yours,

SIMEON STYLITES.

Reading from Left to Right

Sir: From left to right — that's the way the caption always goes with a group photograph, whether it is the high school football team or the solid matrons of the Eastern Star in their best clothes and hair-dos. You read from left to right to find out which is Mrs. Smith and which is Mrs. Jones, though it is often hard to tell the difference.

Is it only cantankerousness that makes me long, for once, to read from right to left, just for variety? Perhaps the reason for such a longing is that the photographic phrase, "reading from left to right," has disturbing suggestions. It is not only group photographs but individual lives that so often read "from left to right." That is, a person who at the age of twenty is lined up away over on the left in social and economic matters, after the age of forty is likely to be discovered clear over on the right. Eddie Whosis, who terrified his mother and the school principal as the demon secretary of the Young Socialist League, reaches sailor's snug harbor at the age of forty-five as secretary of the Chamber of Commerce. The Reverend Hector Boanerges, the problem child of his official board as the vehement ministerial member of the Trade Union Council, at the age of fifty turns up as a member of the Advisory Council of Spiritual Mobilization.

Left to right! Left to right! I'd like to find some biographies that read from right to left as the years roll by. Miss Imogene Brown, for instance, who starts out as the recording secretary of the Dolly Madison Chapter of the D.A.R. and ends up as a candidate for alderman on the American Labor ticket. Must a life always be a reading from left to right?

I suppose there are many reasons for the movement to the right. Obviously one factor is what we read about in the news from Europe, the "dollar shortage." One man explained his movement by saying that he grew more conservative with every set of twins. A current definition is: A liberal is a radical with a wife and two children. There is a mystery wrapped up in the common phrase, "tired liberals." Who ever heard of a "tired conservative"? Why is it always the liberals

who get tired? I would give 64 cents for an anwer to
that question.

What happens to so many white-headed boys of liberal causes that they travel from left to right? Can
anyone remember when Mark Sullivan was a mad
Bull Moose, breathing fire and slaughter? What happened to John Chamberlain? Or John Dos Passos?

At any rate, I am out to collect biographies, if any,
of folks whose lives move from right to left. Here is an
attractive design for living from the age of eighty onward. It is in the words of a pilgrim who kept his flag
flying to the end, Don Marquis: *

We hold by standards, rules and norms.
But when I'm eighty I intend
To turn a fool again for twenty years or so;
Go back to being twenty-five,
Drop caution and conventions, join some little group
Fantastically rebel and alive
And revolute from soup
To nuts; I'll reimburse myself
For all the freak stuff that I've had to keep upon the
    shelf;
Indulge my crotchets, be a friend of man,
And pull the thoughts I've always had to can.
I'm looking forward to a rough, rebellious, unrespect-
    able old age,
Kicking the world uphill

* From *Noah an' Jonah an' Cap'n John Smith* by Don Marquis. Copyright, 1921, D. Appleton and Company. Reprinted
by permission of the publishers Appleton-Century-Crofts, Inc.

With laughter shrill
And squeals of high-pitched throaty rage.
                    Yours,

                              SIMEON STYLITES.

A Partridge in a Pear Tree

Sir: With Christmas coming up, may I remind you
that there is no carol that offers more fun for a few
people singing together, whether they can sing or not,
than the old stand-by "The Twelve Days of Christmas." There is a fine lilt to it, and the fascination that
children of all ages find in a cumulative song on the
model of "The House that Jack Built," where the list
of things to be remembered and repeated gets longer
with each stanza and you get all out of breath and have
a grand time.

It is an old and universal carol, in celebration of the
twelve days from Christmas to Epiphany. You know
it —

> *On the first day of Christmas*
> *My true love gave to me*
> *A partridge in a pear tree.*

Then it goes on with a list of the most riotously inappropriate and ludicrous gifts — two turtle doves,
three French hens, six geese laying, seven swans sing-

ing, eight maids milking, ending with twelve drummers drumming.

Nonsense? Not by a jugful of wassail. It is a profound philosophy of giving. It celebrates the high wisdom of completely inappropriate and largely useless gifts. And a good thing to remember just before Christmas. A partridge in a pear tree — what on earth could one do with that? That's the beauty of it! That makes it something to sing about! And folks have been singing about it for several hundred years. Would they have sung about a floor mop (highly appropriate for housecleaning) or a tea kettle or a foot warmer? Not much!

So take a suggestion for your shopping list. Give your true love an inappropriate gift. Don't get grandma another lace cap or pair of woolen mittens. She has plenty already, and besides she hates the things. Get her a little bottle of Chanel No. 5 or a set of lipsticks or a pair of dancing slippers. That will boost her morale, make her feel she is still alive. As you reach for that fine book for your beloved pastor, the learned tome *Archaeology and the Bible*, stay your hand. Reach over to the next counter and get him the *New Yorker Book of Cartoons*. There will be several cartoons by Peter Arno, highly inappropriate for the clergy. That's the idea. There are few joys greater than that of stepping out of character for a time. And I'll bet it will do a lot more for his sermons too. And father — lay off the neckties and the conservative scarf. Get him a Lionel electric train, appropriate for age nine. (All his own; Junior keep away!)

Dad has always had a yen for one. And for your wife —
well, that has me stumped, as usual. How about a — er
— ah — Oh well, how about a partridge in a pear tree?
It would be a surprise.

The best gifts of love are those which show a lovely
lack of common sense. Flowers (they fade, don't they?),
a bracelet (invariably a nuisance). It is usually on the
twenty-fifth anniversary that a husband gives a vacuum
cleaner or a Mix Master.

There is high precedent for all this. The first Christ-
mas gift was highly inappropriate — a Baby in a barn.
Who wanted that? No one clapped his hands and said,
"Goody, goody, just what I wanted!" That is, no one
except a few souls who could really see — Simeon and
Anna in the Temple, some shepherds, His mother.

> *They were all looking for a king*
> *To slay their foes and lift them high.*
> *Thou cam'st a little baby thing*
> *To make a woman cry.*

Yours with a sprig of holly,
SIMEON STYLITES.

Wise Men from the West

Sir: I heard the words being read, "In the days of
Herod the King, behold, Wise Men from the East
came to Jerusalem . . ." Then my mind, never very

strong at sticking to the point, trailed off. Suppose, I thought, suppose that the Wise Men had come from the West rather than from the East. Suppose, too, that they shared and expressed some of the main, dominant ideas and drives of our Western civilization and world. What would have happened if it had been Wise Men from the West journeying eastward toward a star? The extracanonical scriptures might have read like this:

The First Wise Man, being a top ruler in the Western world, was a merchant prince, a big industrialist, ever alert to the opportunity of bigger and better sales. At the start of the journey he said to himself: "We are going to be traveling through large, untapped markets. I can follow the star and at the same time open up new outlets for the Caspar Manufacturing Company and triple our exports." So he diligently called on all the tradesmen along the way. He amassed a big sheaf of orders. But it all took time and delayed him greatly, so that the star faded and he never got to Bethlehem at all.

The Second Wise Man had a true Western feeling for military power and defense. He said to himself: "We will be traveling through foreign nations and strange peoples. The gifts we bear will need armed protection. I must recruit a strong force and arm them well. Otherwise we will never get to Jerusalem." But the recruiting and problems of logistics took time, and his soldiers were always getting into brawls with the soldiers of the nations through which they passed. Rome refused to allow such a menacing task force to pass through Italy. So they did not get any farther than Gaul, where they went into winter quarters.

The Third Wise Man was very different from the other two, in everything except his vision of the star and the desire to find the King. But he too was a true man of Western culture and aims. He had been called many harsh things by rivals, but no one had ever called him a shrinking violet. He had a high position — no less than president of Melchior, Melchior, Melchior & Melchior, Advertising and Public Relations Consultants. He said to himself: "This finding of a new King will be a tremendously big thing. It has great publicity possibilities and must be handled in a big way. We will be marching right into history and the whole world must get the full story." So he was much engaged in giving out press releases at every town at which they stopped, and entertaining local journalists. For the sake of complete coverage he made a detour into Egypt, which took three months. But by that time the King of the Jews had been born at Bethlehem, and he never got to see the King at all or to present his gifts.

Perhaps it is just as well that the Wise Men came from the East. Perhaps the West, with all its power and skill, still misses the way to the Star and the Babe in Swaddling Clothes.

Yours,

SIMEON STYLITES.

A Squeeze of the Lemon

Sir: As I have boasted to you before, every other year I read a book. Last year it was a novel. I can't remember the name, but there was one bit in it which spoke to my condition and was worth the price of admission. A woman in London, after the close of the war, remarked to her husband, "Won't it be wonderful now that we can give up quietly radiating confidence and good cheer, and can settle back into being our grumbling, acid selves."

Perhaps that was greeted by me as a needed justification for making sour remarks. But I am sure that most of us welcome the passing of the necessity of radiating good cheer or anything noble. It is like taking off tight shoes and putting on your old slippers; like the command "At ease" to a buck private after a five-mile fatigue march.

There are many more endearing characters than the professional "radiator" of goodness. Too much sugar is not good for the body — or for conversation. Continuous good cheer and uplift can be hard to take. Maybe that is the reason one man said he never liked the clergy "in bulk." Tea is improved by a little lemon; and a squeeze of the lemon, a bit of sharp, astringent tartness, adds much to the interest of life and conversation. Some good people always seem to have a faint odor of tuberoses in their conversation, calling for the restrained decorum of a funeral. Perhaps Wordsworth liked a flavor of lemon; hence his description of the ideal woman:

> *A creature not too bright or good*
> *For human nature's daily food.*

An irritated squeeze of the lemon makes even the saints human. What did St. Theresa ever say that draws us more to her than her exclamation when caught in a thunder-storm, "O Lord, it is no wonder that you have so few friends if this is the way you treat them!" You wouldn't mind having a saint like that living next door, or even dropping in to dinner.

A bit of lemon flavor now and then keeps life from being a pose. It was an authentic saint of the nineteenth century, Alexander Whyte of Edinburgh, who wrote: "We are too formal. We have too much starch in our souls. Starch is more deadly than sin. Your soul may be saved from sin, but scarcely from starch." There is sure scientific basis for that in physiological chemistry, in that sugar easily turns into starch. Saved from starch — that is a miracle and a blessed one.

And how the lemon keeps life interesting! How the mind rejoices in the two lovely squeezes of the lemon administered by Bernard Shaw and Winston Churchill. Shaw sent Churchill two tickets for the opening night of one of his plays, along with a note: "Come and bring a friend, if you have one." Mr. Churchill wrote back that he could not come on the opening night, but would come on the second night, "if there is a second night." Tie score!

The chief objection to continuous sugar is that it never lets us get detached enough to criticize our world, because it never lets us get detached enough to see it. We should go Matthew Arnold one better: Sweetness and light — and a squeeze of the lemon!

Yours,

SIMEON STYLITES.

The Blood of the Martyrs

Sir: Shortly after New Year's I received a church bulletin which contained a note from the pastor to the congregation that moved me deeply, as accounts of truly great heroes always stir the soul. In his note the pastor expressed his joy and pride in the members of the congregation who had "braved the rain" in order to attend the service on Christmas morning.

Just let that picture sink into your imagination. Earnest Christians, on the high festal day of their faith, nobly daring the raindrops, some no doubt even lifting umbrellas, and resolutely walking out to the garage, climbing into the car, and coming to church. Evidently such valor merits a Te Deum. Who says the race is sinking down which owns lads and lasses like that?

Truly such martyrdom calls to mind earlier martyrs,

who "conquered kingdoms, enforced justice, received promises, stopped the mouths of lions, quenched raging fire, escaped the edge of the sword, won strength out of weakness, became mighty in war, put foreign armies to flight."

The pastor's tribute to those who "braved the rain" suggests a Roll of Modern Protestant Martyrs who performed comparable exploits of faith. Time would fail us to tell the deeds of Gideon, Barak, Samson; it would fail us also to recite the record of some heroisms of our day.

There is Polycarp Brown, for instance, who came to the morning service once every three months, on fine Sundays, and stayed all through to the benediction. Hell's foundations tremble when shaken by devotion like that.

There is St. Teresa Robinson, who, it is true, did not stop the mouths of lions, but did stop the mouths of patrons of the Ladies Aid suppers, having made pies four times in one year.

There is Pierpont Morton, who increased his subscription to the church from $2 to $3 a Sunday, and was fittingly rewarded by another deduction from his income tax.

There is Barnabas Cox, who with unvarying fidelity attended the Easter service and the annual meeting every year; and Demos Duval, who attended two Men's Club dinners and even played end man in the Minstrel Show.

There is Mrs. Boanerges Johnson, who during the

fall and winter drove her two children seven blocks to Sunday school, called for them at 11 a.m. and drove them home again. Of such is the Kingdom of Heaven.

Surely the blood of the martyrs is the seed of the church, today as in the far yesterday. Such martyrdoms as these promise a great harvest for the church of to-morrow.

> *They climbed the steep ascent of heaven*
> *Through peril, toil and pain.*

Yours,

SIMEON STYLITES.

In Absentia

Sir: Back in June courtesy demanded that I attend several commencement exercises at which the promising offspring of some of my neighbors received degrees and presents. My friends were just the right emotional distance from me — near enough to make it a glad occasion, but not close enough to demand a graduation present.

I noticed that several graduates were awarded their degrees *in absentia.* They were not there, but they got the diploma anyhow. Even one LL.D. did not get into the act; he was *in absentia.* (At one college as the orator of the day explained the world situation *in extenso,* I wished that I were *in absentia* myself.)

Then I began to wonder idly whether one of the thousand predicaments of the world might not lie in the fact that too many people not only graduate, but *live,* for the most part, *in absentia.* They are not "all there." Of course, their mental faculties have standard equipment and, if properly oiled, could be in good running order. But for all practical purposes their brains and attention are *in absentia.* When an occasion rises demanding complete attention or — horrors! — steady thinking, their theme song is, "My heart's in the highlands, my heart is not here." So they live in what William James said was a baby's first mental habitat, "a buzzing, blooming blur." Through that scene they walk withdrawn in an absent air.

For such unemployed minds the worn clichés, the smooth nickels of speech are a wonderful boon. They can be tossed back and forth, like tennis balls over a net, in a half-hour's conversation without disturbing a bit of gray matter. Some very engaging portraits of women talking *in absentia* have been drawn, all the way from Mrs. Malaprop to Gracie Allen. That is unfair, for the minds of men are just as often A.W.O.L. When the roll is called, not up yonder but down here, wouldn't it be a help if a few million more people could answer with a firm "Present"?

But what I started to write is this (I have been *in absentia* myself): Isn't one of the biggest handicaps of the churches the obvious one that too many members are every Sunday literally *in absentia?* They are not present. Recall that as a prelude to the biggest event in the history of the church, its Birthday, Pentecost, we read: "They went up to the upper room . . . and all these with one accord devoted themselves to prayer." That is the indispensable prelude to any real birthday, to any new birth — for the church to be in accord in one place, instead of seventeen places with seventeen varieties of nonaccord.

If the habits of that company in the upper room had been like the habits of multitudes in our churches today, the record would be a sorry entry like this:

The meeting was called for the first day of the week, but so many things interfered that of the company of 120, only 40 could be present. Peter and his wife had bought a cottage on Lake Galilee and were away from the hot city over the weekend. Bartholomew had guests and of course could not come. Philip and his family had been up late the night before and overslept. Andrew had a business conference about a new fishing boat. James had to stay at home and cut the grass, which had grown long.

No Pentecost!

See you in church.

Yours,

SIMEON STYLITES.

'What Have You Been Doing, Then?'

Sir: One of the most embarrassing questions ever asked appears on an enchanted page of a magic book, *The Wind in the Willows,* by Kenneth Grahame. The Mole is talking to the Water Rat.

" 'Do you know, I've never been in a boat before in all my life,' said the Mole.

" 'What?' cried the Rat, open-mouthed: 'Never been in a — you never — well I — *what have you been doing, then?*' "

That is the embarrassing question. If you missed this part of the Big Show, what have you been doing? For instance, have you ever read *The Wind in the Willows?* No? What have you been doing, then? And the Rat had a good question: If you have never been in a boat, what on earth . . . ? Some people don't like boats, and shun rowboats, sailboats, any boats, poor creatures. What have they been doing? If you have never tipped over in a canoe, it is almost as bad as never having been baptized.

Have you been to the zoo lately? Then, what on earth have you been doing? The zoo is a reinforcement of faith; it persuades you that the Lord has a sense of humor, and so things will work out all right. Isn't the zebra a proof that the Creator has a keen sense of humor? Or the giraffe? Or, much nearer home, the duck? F. W. Harvey was literally inspired in his version of Creation: *

*And as for the duck, I think God must have smiled a
    bit,*
*Seeing those bright eyes blink on the day he fashioned
    it.*
*And he's probably laughing still, at the sound that
    came out of its bill.*

In other words, we need more minor ecstasies than most of us get — "bits of star dust," as they have been called. It is true, of course, that we need major ecstasies too, such as can be found in love and religion. Emily Dickinson had it measured rightly: †

> *Take all away from me,*
> *But leave me ecstasy.*

That is the trouble with the religion of many people. There is never any ecstasy, no hop, skip, and jump, just a dutiful trudge.

Gardening is a good minor ecstasy. (I am safe in referring to my gardening exploits, since my wife never reads my stuff and will thus not contradict me. That seems a bit unfair in her. I drink her coffee when it is literally not so hot; she ought to read my stuff when it is in the same condition.) A garden is a great excite-

* Reprinted by permission of Sidgwick & Jackson, Ltd.
† From *Poems of Emily Dickinson,* edited by M. Dickinson Bionchi and A. L. Hampson, reprinted by permission of the publisher, Little, Brown & Company.

ment — just planting a tulip bulb and then wonder whether a cauliflower will come up or only witch grass. If you don't garden, what *have* you been doing?

How about the 48 per cent of all people who, the survey sharks tell us, never read a book in a year? What have *they* been doing? It doesn't make any difference. They have missed the Big Show. They never travel in the realms of gold. They just go by bus or the 8:15. That is not travel; it is just transportation — quite a different thing.

> *He danced along the dingy days,*
> *And this bequest of wings*
> *Was but a book.**

But some people never dance. They walk solemnly and arthritically toward the cemetery.

Pick out a good minor ecstasy before you petrify.

Yours,

SIMEON STYLITES.

Cadenza

Sir: One of the blessings of ignorance — I have much to be thankful for — is that many things wise folk have known for years come to you as an amazing, joyful surprise. I have just discovered one of the loveliest words in the dictionary, whose meaning has been foggy

* From *Poems of Emily Dickinson,* edited by M. Dickinson Bionchi and A. L. Hampson, reprinted by permission of the publisher, Little, Brown & Company.

for a long time. It is a beautiful word, with a beautiful idea set in it like a jewel. It is the word "cadenza," which I learn from the dictionary means "that portion of a concerto where the soloist is permitted to build some fanciful improvisations upon the straight musical facts which confront him."

There have been tricky cadenzas by Kreisler, Menuhin, and a hundred others, graceful melodious little dances on the strings, but not to be found in the notes on the score sheet.

I do not know how we could live without cadenzas, especially when the facts we are confronted with are pretty bare.

The cadenza is the refuge of childhood against a world of dull facts. Children as a tribe do not lie. They make cadenzas, "improvisations on the facts which confront them." On the street they see a bus and a dog. But what sort of food is that to nourish the emotional life of a growing child? So they do a little cadenza; they report seeing two grizzly bears, or, on red letter days, a deer. With highly gifted children there is even sometimes an elephant. That adds to the joy of life.

Some foolish parents punish their children for such improvisation. Such parents should be reported to the Society for the Prevention of Cruelty to Children.

Too many people seem to take as their life motto the words of the poker-faced detective in the Dragnet television program: "I want the facts, ma'am, just want the facts." So they live on facts and never bring any music out of life more thrilling than Chop Sticks.

There is an old story with a lot of wisdom to it

about two cowboys who were snowbound for the winter in the mountains. Each had one book which he read continually. One had "One Thousand and One Interesting Facts." The other had Omar Khayyam. When spring came, they went down to Texas and both courted the same girl. One would say, "Miss Louisa, did you know that the Brooklyn Bridge is 5,678 feet long?" The next night the other, drawing on his winter's study, would say:

> *Here with a loaf of Bread beneath the Bough,*
> *A Flask of Wine, a Book of Verse — and Thou*
> *Beside me singing in the Wilderness,*
> *And Wilderness were Paradise enow.*

Louisa plunked for Omar. And wisely. He could do a cadenza on the facts.

Many people have lived in a town that was a collection of dreary facts — from the car window. Not even any mute inarticulate Miltons. But they have made improvisation, and have brought excitement and romance to life that was a lot truer than "the facts." Others have made lilting music that was not in the score of a grim and rugged job. Charles Lamb might have written the story of his life under the title, "Thirty-Five Years on a Stool" in the East India office. Instead, he improvised on the facts and wrote immortal cadenzas.

Faith is really a cadenza. Here were the facts of St. Paul's life: "Often at the point of death . . . five times have I got forty lashes, three times have I been

beaten by the Romans . . . once pelted with stones
. . . three times shipwrecked . . . starving many a
time, cold and ill-clad . . ."

Bleak facts! Here is the improvisation he made on
the facts: "He makes my life a constant pageant of
triumph!"

Yours,

SIMEON STYLITES.

'I Played Their Accompaniment'

Sir: It was almost the only book in the place, so I almost read it. It gave a good close-up of a demanding
profession — *I Played Their Accompaniment,* by
Elizabeth Barbison David. For many years the author
played the accompaniment for concert singers, such as
Schumann-Heink, Geraldine Farrar, and Tetrazzini.
It is a difficult and delicate art. A big part of it is the
exacting business of subordination, to hold oneself
the unobtrusive servant of another's art, in phrasing,
accent, and timing, watching the face, the breathing,
the volume of sound.

This art has no spotlight or applause. The accom-
panist succeeds just in proportion as he is forgotten. In
that profession, surely, he that loseth his life shall find
it. Now if I were a pianist, instead of a baffled Bee-
thoven or a suppressed Schubert, the notice in the
paper would be something like this: "Occasionally the

rich voice of Marian Anderson could be heard faintly above the ferocious pounding on the piano by a man designed by nature to be a blacksmith, a certain Mr. Stylites."

It is a great role. It has been historically a mother's role. She doesn't sing the song or get the applause; she merely makes it possible. At a college commencement a few years ago, where a young man was graduated with high honors, there was in the audience a great musician, his mother. For years she had rendered notable music on two remarkable musical instruments, a typewriter and a washboard, the melodious accompaniment which made his education possible.

It has been so often a woman's role. Whenever great music is rendered in life the direction frequently applies,"*Cherchez la femme.*" The classic instance, oft retold, is that of the wife of Wendell Phillips. When he went out to the rough-and-tumble of an Abolition meeting she did not say, "Now for heaven's sake, Wendell, don't make a fool of yourself and say something to stir up trouble." No, what she said was, "Don't shilly-shally, Wendell." Quite a musical note!

And men have played a subordinated accompaniment. A friend of one of the greatest figures in American life a few years ago heard him refer to his brother Ralph. The friend said in surprise, "I didn't know you had a brother Ralph." The man replied, "No one else did either. He stayed at home and ran the farm, so that the rest of us could go to college."

Such music from the background is not a consolation prize; it is a great achievement. In different form Edward Arlington Robinson put it. "I know that the themes of William Vaughn Moody are not for me," he wrote in a letter. "I must be content with a jew's-harp and a bass drum, and let the other fellow play the trumpet."

This goes into a much wider circumference. In the United Nations, many are trying to render worldwide music on other instruments than guns and bombs. It will not be rendered without the accompaniment of millions of people.

Yours in B-sharp minor,

SIMEON STYLITES.

Advertising Witchcraft

Sir: Is yours a normal American home? Do you have radio and TV? Or are you still one of the early settlers of Chicago, leading the simple life of the frontier?

If you have those helps to modern living, you have doubtless noticed how the advertising profession has in these days taken up magic and witchcraft. The simple announcements of good merchandise which marked primitive days are far behind.

Today it is not enough to say, "This is a good tooth-paste. Brush your teeth with it hard and often enough and it will help to keep your teeth clean." Heavens, no! No one cares about prosaic stuff like that. Get in some magic. Try witchcraft and incantations like "Abracadabra."

So the modern trend is to claim some magic ingredient which can be introduced with potent hocus-pocus. This is the pattern you can hear a dozen times on a TV evening: "Squeezy Toothpaste is the greatest magic since Grimm's Fairy Tales. It has a new magic ingredient named, 'Hold Everything.' If you have had any teeth pulled out, a thirty-day test of Squeezy will restore them, though, to be frank, it will take in some cases sixty days to restore wisdom teeth."

Nearly every product has its own bit of witchcraft, a spell which protects it from all ills. Thus, in these lung-cancer days, the cigaret boys have a new line of magic, something very close to this: "Of course, if you smoke any other brand of cigaret than Hyenas, you will drop dead. But Hyenas have a new ingredient, X B 24, the greatest achievement of science since the discovery of gravitation, which will screen out the poison and leave you only flavor, or nothing at all."

The gasolines fall in line. Often the claim is made that not only is Ethyl added but a magic ingredient is put into Block Buster Special which gives it less non-fermented sugar than any other gasoline. Or am I getting this mixed up?

One dairy in the middle west advertises its milk as ready to use. Evidently no other cows can make that statement.

At this rate it will not be long before the public-relations wizards of southern resorts can give up too great reliance on bathing beauties and plug for a new ingredient in their special air. Their atmosphere is no longer ordinary NO^3, merely nitrogen and oxygen, which is very commonplace and probably bad for the lungs. It has added a new, marvelous factor, called by scientists 3.1416 — something out of this world. Do not die in the north! Come on down south!

Progress is wonderful. But sometimes, in the midst of all the noise, I wonder if many of the customers these days really believe in magic and witchcraft. What do you think?

Yours,

SIMEON STYLITES.

Irregular

Sir: The hymnals I like best are those which have little musical directions at the top of the page, indicating how the hymn should be played and sung. Not that it makes much vocal difference to me. I cannot aspire to fulfilling the injunction to "make a *joyful* noise unto the Lord"; it is all pretty doleful. But I can obey the command in the 98th Psalm, "Make a *loud* noise and rejoice."

Just the same, the musical directions enliven your thoughts. I have always been startled by the musical direction which goes with the hymn "Onward Christian Soldiers" — "May be sung in unison." Exactly!

It had *better* be sung in unison! The loveliest one of all is the direction which goes with the Christmas carol "There's a song in the air, There's a star in the sky." The direction reads, "Irregular." I should say so! The whole thing was highly irregular! A Baby in a barn. What could be more irregular than that? Shockingly irregular!

Two thoughts, decked with holly for Christmas, come out of this musical notation. We have in Christianity a most irregular religion. We worship a most irregular God. His ways are past finding out. Anything can happen. The worst enemies of vital Christianity are those who have tried to regularize it, to take out its fantastic, peculiar qualities and leave it no different from anything else. Thus, often, a company called to be disturbers have dwindled down into a company of regular fellows, achieving the fine regularity of the cemetery.

Here's the other thought — a Baby in a barn! There was a place in the organized life of Judea in which babies might be born. It was not a barn. But there was no room in the inn, so a barn was used. God never gets to the end of his rope. If there is no room in the fitting place, he uses another, even a manger.

There is a place for every new revelation of God to be born. That place is God's church. But if there is no room in the church — as there has often been no room — God can find a barn or other place in which his new word can be born.

There was a time in the early nineteenth century

for a new revelation of the meaning of the Christian gospel. That was while the slaughter of the innocents was going on, a slaughter of children, often mere babies, in mine and factory, which made Herod's little exploit in killing look like pretty small stuff. When the Ten Hours bill, limiting the labor of children to ten hours a day, was introduced in Parliament the Bishops of the Church of England, who had seats in the House of Lords, voted overwhelmingly against it. You can see the godly bishops, "goodly in girth," protesting fervently against the weak sentimentalism of allowing the children of the poor to get off with a mere ten hours a day at work.

There was no room in the inn of the church, so that baby was born in a barn. There were of course individual Christians, such as Shaftesbury, who led in the fight. But the new insight into the rights of childhood came from labor rather than in the institution where such new insights might be expected to originate.

The inn was full, but that did not stop the incarnation. There is need for new revelations of the meaning of the Christian message. Will they come in the church or in a barn?

Yours,

SIMEON STYLITES.

How To Be a Bad Parent

Sir: The Parent-Teacher Association of the John L. Sullivan School got so hard pressed to fill out their program for the year that they had to put Simeon into one of the slots. The secretary who wrote me said, "Just talk on anything that you know something about." Poor innocent dear, she did not realize what a formidable restriction that was. But I came up with a topic on which I am a real authority — "How To Be a Bad Parent."

One way to be a bad parent is not to get any fun out of the job. That tops them all. We live in antiseptic and homogenized days — and nights — when for every sterilized bottle in the refrigerator there is a book of baby lore on the shelf. Many parents are so weighed down by the responsibility of keeping Junior on schedule to the split second, and keeping his little soul from being scarred by frustration, that they become two young philosophers with a worried look instead of a couple of amateurs having the time of their lives. It is an axiom, to me at least, that the amount of good a person can do depends greatly on how much fun he gets out of it. Parents might well stop and laugh at the preposterous idea that they should be the guardians of an immortal soul. But they have no time for fun.

We went on a picnic one summer with a young couple who brought along an item, aged one. The picnic turned out not an adventure in delight but a problem in logistics; they had brought enough apparatus to fit out an army. Nobody had much fun; there was something to do every five minutes; and the baby did not get to eat any ants at all.

Then there is the type of parent, usually, alas, the father, who is the Nervous-Wreck Parent. Generally the husky brute does not look like a nervous wreck, but he likes the role. The mother's theme song is: "Quiet, children! Your father has had a hard day at the office. No, Imogene, he cannot read you 'The Three Bears.' Willie, stop that drumming, it makes father nervous."

Then there is the Bronze Statue type of parent, like the Civil War soldiers that stand immobile in nearly every town in the country, having endured undisturbed the onslaught of close to a hundred winters. Many parents have the same degree of warmth and spontaneity. They look down with either calm benignity or the remoteness of a figure in bronze.

And don't forget the Run-Along Parent. This type saves a lot of time and trouble. "Mamma, why do puppy dogs' tails curl?" "Oh, run along, dear." "Where does the sun go when it goes down?" "Run along, dear." Those are deadly words. Like a blight-

ing frost they kill a beautiful flower, a child's imagination. The child asks for the bread of some intelligent
conversation and gets the stone of "run along."

Time for me to run along, too.

Yours,

SIMEON STYLITES.

Somebody Must Sell Suspension Bridges

Sir: My total recall is slipping. A long time ago I read
a story, but in the intervening years a heavy fog has
blown in and I have only a dim picture even of the
point which the story made.

It was a story about a salesman, energetic, enthusias-
tic, hopeful. He left home every day eager to go out
and sell the goods. But he found a lot of consumer resistance. He had a good line, too — selling suspension
bridges. When he came home at night his wife would
ask him skeptically, "Well, did you sell any suspension
bridges today?" He always had to make the disheart-
ened answer, "No, the market is slow." Finally his wife
would give him a little heart-to-heart talk: "Why don't
you sell something that people want? Nobody on Main
Street is in the market for a suspension bridge. Why
don't you switch to soap or razor blades or nylon
stockings? Then we might eat regularly."

Here is where my memory slips. I think the end was
that the poor man saw the point and took up some
brisk selling item, and they lived happily ever after.

Or somewhat happily. For deep in the salesman's mind was the conviction, not to be downed, which he repeated from time to time: "But somebody must sell suspension bridges."

Now of course the wife interested in eating had a point. It is easier to sell articles of immediate practical use and low price than to sell a rainbow. College students learned that lesson. Back in the stone age, when Simeon was in college, students tried to sell many things in low demand. Simeon spent a hot summer trying to sell to farmers, *The Colossal Book of Facts*, $4.98 in the cloth binding. He got personally acquainted with every dog in southern Illinois. The farmers were not hungering for facts. In later years wiser students sold what every woman wanted, silk stockings or aluminum, so that the only question was the price.

But the salesman's conviction, "Somebody must sell suspension bridges," has a bigger point. It is part of the eternal debate between the easy, the immediately practical and cheap, and the more remote, costly, and basic thing. Mr. Chesterton said that if there is some minor trouble with an engine a mechanic can fix it, but if there is anything radically wrong with it you have to drag some theoretician out of a laboratory. The debate has gone on in medicine. Of course somebody must make and sell aspirin and liniment. But, more than that, somebody must do cancer and polio research.

In the world today somebody must sell suspension bridges. There is a tremendous gap between the actual world on the dizzy edge of disaster and the potential world of order. A bridge must be thrown across the chasm by which nations can get from here to there alive. It is much easier to sell immediate, "practical" things, such as guns and bombs and planes that will do 700 miles an hour. Added to that is the difficulty that bridges are suspect. We in America have about reached the point where anything that really goes to the heart of the world's predicament is subversive. To many people it seems much wiser to blow up the abutments of the bridges to international order that have been laid.

The oldest joke in New York city is the one about confidence men selling the Brooklyn bridge. It is no joke any longer. Somebody must sell bridges to reach across chasms of conflict. Run this advertisement in your paper, please.

> *WANTED. Ten million salesmen for Suspension Bridges. No immediate salary, but a large commission.*

Yours,

SIMEON STYLITES.

Heresy

Sir: There are so many orthodoxies imposed from above these days that it is probably a waste of time to get all hot and bothered about any of the minor ones. Still, when you get mad it is well to let it off some way. And I'm mad. So here goes a left hook (not, I am sorry to say, very murderous) against a literary dictatorship today which is spoiling novels for 90 per cent of the customers.

This relentless orthodoxy decrees that novels, to be worth noticing at all, must deal with abnormal types of people; they must be earnest festivals of despair, gaily decorated with the funeral black of fashionable pessimism, a blackout where no false ray of sunshine ever gets in. Reading a novel used to be fun. Now it is a visit to a psychiatric clinic.

Do you think I am just raving? Look at a couple of samples of what I mean, right from the top Sanhedrin. Here is a well-established critic, John W. Aldridge, the author of *After the Lost Generation,* reviewing a recent novel, *The Deep Sleep,* by Wright Morris. Mr. Aldridge thus starts the cheering over the appearance of a "sinister note":

> The author in the past has frequently been crippled by too much loving compassion . . . Lately a new and healthier sinister note has crept into Mr. Morris' novels . . . His charming native types, his average husbands and wives, have grown slightly monstrous; his homely domestic circles have come to resemble the lairs of female animals strewn with the carcasses of men. What was once warming to the heart is now chilling,

and with the change Mr. Morris has acquired
new meaning and stature as a novelist. [*The New
York Times,* Sept. 11, 1953.]

So help me, that's what the man said. Wow! That's
literature with a large L. Notice the high spots: "a
healthier sinister note" — the dumb clucks of average
wives and husbands delightfully changed into mon-
sters; the stature of a novelist measured by "chilling
the heart."

Here is another High Priest of the Temple of Criticism, Mr. Robert Lidell, in his book, *Some Principles
of Fiction:*

> What we demand of an author is rather, per-
> haps, a feeling of sadness, a lack of faith in simple
> and easy solutions to human problems, a sense of
> the frailty of life . . . No loud hearty songs of
> innocence, but quiet songs of experience. And a
> great part of the experience of our time is ex-
> pressed in a few sad little words of Mr. Stephen
> Spender's:
>
> > "*Who live under the shadow of a war,
> > What can I do that matters?*"

There we are! What can we do? Nothing. Let's all go
down and jump in the river! The above quotation, by
the way, is the most arrant sentimentalism imaginable.

We know that life is no Daisy Chain or Hoop-
Rolling Festival. But we submit that most people
have suspected that by this time; and for the novelist

to shout it out is no more news than for a paper boy to come yelling down the street, "Extra! Extra! Caesar Invades Gaul!"

If that is orthodoxy — and it is, in many top critical circles — then I am a heretic, damned from here to eternity and glad of it. Will you join me in a literary Fourth of July and set off a 25-cent giant cracker as a Declaration of Literary Independence? Too many novels bow to this pattern:

My father's vest is stained with bits of egg.
My mother, drunk, sits sobbing in her tea.
Young Michael's kicking sister in the leg,
While mad desire stirs restlessly in me.

"Here's truth indeed," the younger critics cry.
"This man sees life, and, seeing, dares to write." . . .
But as I read their words I faintly sigh,
And wish that God had given them better sight.

So do I.

Yours,

SIMEON STYLITES.

The Man Who Caught Up with Himself

Sir: Once upon a time there was a man who could never catch up with himself. He never got "even with the board." For twenty years or more he had been chasing himself, and only once or twice did he have even fleeting glimpses of his elusive figure vanishing up the road miles ahead.

He would glance every day at his desk, which looked like the wreck of a railway mail car. It was piled high with unanswered letters, and papers about which he should have done something — heaven knows what — two weeks ago. For relief, he would step to the window and look out on the beautiful world, in which he could plainly see that the grass needed cutting badly and the car needed washing badly and the bushes should have been trimmed last spring. Sticking his tongue in the cavity of a molar, unfilled because he could never catch up with himself to go to the dentist, he would glance down on the top letter of the chaos. It was a greeting from the Second National Bank, calling attention to an overlooked overdraft of $11.72 and discreetly suggesting that he drop in and see the receiving teller, who would be happy to greet him.

Then his wife would enter for a moment of domestic felicity, announcing that *something must be done* about the leak in the roof and that the hot water faucet was having another nervous breakdown. He would go through the ritual about doing something drastic when he got caught up with himself a bit.

One night, after a breathless day at the store, trying to overtake some of the things overdue from last week, he sank down on the pillow with the usual sigh, "If only once, for twenty minutes in twenty years, I could catch up with myself!" Then he slept, and behold, he dreamed a dream.

He was in a beautiful room, with a half-acre of shining mahogany desk before him on which there was not a single letter or scrap of paper. Through the window he could see the trimmed lawn outside, and the washed car, gleaming like the colored advertisements in the slick magazines. No bills, no dates, no nothing. No more foot races with himself. He had caught up with himself. Peace, perfect peace. Or was it? For around the edges of the peaceful vacuum there nibbled a little question: "What do I do now?"

Seeing a postman pass by, he hailed him. He noticed that the postman had no letters or papers in his bag. Nothing to deliver; just out for a walk.

"Where am I?" asked the man.

"This is hell," replied the postman cheerily.

Perhaps it was at that. All caught up; nothing to chase.

Yours,

SIMEON STYLITES.

Calamity by Flood

Sir: The many disastrous flash floods in the spring of 1952 caused one catastrophe that has never received the wide attention it deserved. The little town of Meadowbrook in the Dakotas was terribly hard hit.

(Meadowbrook is probably not on your gas station road map.) The rains descended and the floods came and great was the fall of the village. The usually placid brook became a young Niagara Falls. All wires went down — telephone, telegraph, and power wires — and railroad tracks were washed away. The whole region was incommunicado for several days.

Among other crises, this made a terrific problem for Grace Church in the town. It was put completely out of touch with any General Headquarters of the denomination. The congregation was entirely without direction from above about what Special Days had been designated for the next two Sundays. That meant nothing less than that they were "on their own" — a situation without precedent for the past few years.

What could they do? No new Enlistment Day, no Uncles' and Nephews' Day, no Day at all, just a Blank Sunday! Of course, a few houses had radios run on batteries. But headquarters did not get on the radio, and no directives were dropped by plane. Came Thursday, then Friday, and still no word from Nashville or Chicago or New York.

But the church faced the disaster with calm courage. After much discussion about what they should do with a Sunday on their own, one simple soul suggested that they worship God. That was a radical solution, but in the absence of anything else it was adopted. On the undesignated Sunday the preacher spoke on the text, "Be still, and know that I am God." No Quotas were mentioned and no Special Cards were passed out.

Strangely enough, the people liked it. The pastor, evidently a sentimentalist, writes that after two whole Sundays of such a strange interlude they returned to the program of assigned Days and Drives with refreshed spirits and renewed vigor.

Yours,

SIMEON STYLITES.

The Devils Were White

Sir: The Ethiopian Church portrays all the saints as black and all the devils as white. We can readily understand the point of view. For that is not merely a bit of minor ecclesiastical lore, but just about the most important and terrifying fact of our time. Many of the devils in the world have been, and are, white devils.

Not, of course, by the white man's traditions of art. We do not make pictures of Satan with blond hair and blue eyes and a light skin. Once in a while, as in *Faust,* we give the devil a red suit, but that is just to liven up the scene. We never make him white.

The Ethiopian Church has a lot of history on its side. History is full of white devils. The long, revolting story of the African slave trade is a story of white devils. For centuries the forests of Africa rang with the cry, "Run for your lives! The white devils are coming!" They came, and in some years took away a hundred thousand slaves. It is hard to imagine what a stranglehold the slave trade had on the whole enonomy of Great Britain, before the advent of Wilberforce and Clarkson and others. It was as though a monster octopus had swum up the Mersey estuary, where most of the slave ships went out from, and spread its slimy tentacles to grasp every institution — Parliament, the banks, and many churches.

China knew the white devils all too well. In 1839 the Opium War was forced on China by Great Britain to sanction the importation of opium. The white devils wound the chains of opium on multitudes of Chinese, and then took Hongkong for good measure. Shortly after, Christian missionaries began to carry Christian teachings to the heathen Chinese, who were so besotted as to object to opium. The real bill for all that began to come in during the 1940's and 1950's. It is still coming in.

White devils are abroad in South Africa. Many of the worst of them are armed — as has sometimes happened — with a Bible. They are skillful devils, fomenters of chaos as accomplished in the oppression of the black people as any devils that ever took a postgraduate course in Hell. Langston Hughes has summed it up in a few words: *

> I am looking
> For a house in the world

* Reprinted by kind permission of the author.

Where the white shadows
Will not fall.

There is no such house,
Dark brother,
No such house at all.

In these days when we talk so much about the
Ecumenical Church, one good step might be to come
a bit closer to the Ethiopian Church and share its
sharp vision of the color of devils. Perhaps we might
arrange to have fewer white ones, at any rate.

Yours,

SIMEON STYLITES.

Enter the Crocus!

Sir: The little crocus is coming up in the world. That
ought to occasion no surprise, for that is the long suit
of the crocus — coming up through the ground, and
early. But this is something different: the crocus has
finally got into the Bible! It blooms in the 35th chapter
of Isaiah in the new Revised Standard Version. There,
the desert no longer "blossoms as the rose." Instead we
read, "Like the crocus it shall blossom abundantly."
We are sorry to lose the rose, for that phrase "blossom
as the rose" has worked its way into the memory of our
race. But there is at least one rose still left: "I am a
rose of Sharon."

Nevertheless, here is a rousing welcome to the crocus, for it is a perfect symbol of hope and a model for daring action. The crocus is the pioneer of blossoms, the "take a chance" flower. It does not wait till the snow gets off the ground. It pushes up through, and its sword-shaped leaves say, "Get out of the way, iceberg! Spring is coming." Other flowers may sleep till May or June, but the crocus jumps the gun. Salute to the crocus!

We need more crocuses among humans, people who take the first possible — or impossible — chance, even a 1-to-100 shot, at getting something worth while done. The world has moved forward on the ventures of crocus-minded people. When the Apostle Paul sailed across the narrow sea from Asia to Europe, there was to human view not a chance that he could ever make a dent on Europe with the story of a condemned criminal executed in Palestine. The group of insurance companies known as Lloyds of London will insure almost anything. They even offer a policy against twins. But they would not have insured at any premium Paul's venture into Europe. Paul was a crocus, pushing up in the dead of winter.

If men wait till they can bet on a sure thing, the right time never comes. John Jay Chapman said that he had lived a long time and had been associated with many causes, but never with any cause for which the time was right. When Charles Loring Brace started the Society for the Prevention of Cruelty to Children he was dubbed an "officious fool" — in other words, a "crocus" blooming in January.

The cause of peace and the United Nations desperately need crocuses. The time is not ripe for the U.N. So there is a growing chorus over the country, "This is not the time. Let's wait till June. Then, when the battle is won, if it is won, we can make a resounding speech about it."

If the wilderness of war is ever to blossom, it will be with the blooms of the crocus, people who take a chance when there is hardly a speck of chance.

If anyone should read this — blessed thought, but one of those 1-to-100 chances — I hope he or she will turn it over to the flower committee of the church with the suggestion that a bouquet of crocuses will be a fiting decoration for the chancel.

Yours,

SIMEON STYLITES.

One Bang

Sir: In the life of Henry Irving by his grandson, there is an interesting little item of forgotten theatrical history. In the middle of the nineteenth century the right to produce dramatic performances was limited to certain theaters, which had a monopoly. But the bright boys of the theater found a loophole which enabled them to penetrate that formidable obstruction. Plays were forbidden, but the edict did not apply to opera — that is, plays with music; operas were permitted. So, in many places, at the beginning of a play, one of the theater staff gave one loud bang on the piano. That made it an opera. This was the music of the evening, and the play went safely ahead, without benefit of any more superfluous notes. One swallow does not make a summer, but one bang on the piano *did* make an "opera."

I have seemed to hear that one note of music resounding in many places around me. Listen, and you can hear it too! There are a good many one-note patriots. They stand up reverently with head uncovered while the national anthem is being sung, or they face the flag at the service-club luncheon and sing one stanza of "America"; then they are free for the rest of the week, or the season. After sounding that one note they are not so hot about the tougher aspects of citizenship — having conscience sit in when drawing up an income-tax report, or refusing to make unexamined slogans the turntable of the mind. Why spend time on arias and choruses when one note of music will be enough? But it takes more than one note to transform an indifferent neglect of civic responsibility into an opera.

There have been too many one-bang marriages. In some cases the only note of music was the first—"I will." Or a box of candy once a year. So many marriages have dwindled down into a "tired friendship," with the tiredness more evident than the friendship. Likewise the Mother's Day devotees are adepts at the one-note opera. But one carnation a year cannot change a dull chronicle of neglect into a thrilling opera full of high C's.

Churches at Easter are full of the one-bang tribe. Some people, however, are "twicers"; they strike two notes, one at Easter and one at Christmas. William E. Gladstone, back in the nineteenth century, used to describe himself as a "twicer." That meant that he attended divine service twice a Sunday. Today, however, for many, "twicer" means twice a year. They labor under the delusion that hitting one note can make a grand opera out of a mediocre show.

Did not Someone once say, "Not those who say 'Lord! Lord!' [that is, two bangs] but those who do what I say?"

Yours,

SIMEON STYLITES.

Pentagon

Sir: One of the sharpest bits of satire in the delightful comedy, *The Tea House of the August Moon,* is the picture of the little schoolhouse which the American army of occupation is ordered to build in the revered shape of a pentagon. The play presents the adventures of Captain Fishby when he starts out with Plan B,

direct from the Pentagon in Washington, under his
arm, to transform a little village in Okinawa.

The little schoolhouse shaped like a pentagon pictures the greatest weakness of much of the American
approach to the world today. Many of the High Brass
sigh:

> . . . could we with Fate conspire
> To grasp this Sorry Scheme of things entire,
>   Would we not shatter it to bits — and then
> Remold it nearer to the heart's desire!

It would be remolded into the shape of a Pentagon.
That Is the Shape of Things To Come.

Just think for a moment of the Plan B and the blue-
prints for an American village in Okinawa, sprung
fully armed from the mind of Jove in Washington.
No wonder the natives joyfully accepted the plan and
then quietly transformed the schoolhouse into a tea-
house!

Too much Pentagon thinking. Military thinking is
not enough for situations whose complexity runs far
beyond any Manual of Arms. Yet that is the kind of
thinking we are getting in such large and frightening
measure.

A government employee in Washington has been
whispering to his friends a recent bit of history that
he would not dare tell on the street corner; so he shall
be nameless here. A mechanic from the middle west
got a job as a taxicab driver in Washington. About
driving, he knew everything; about Washington, noth-

ing. He took on a passenger at the Union Station, who ordered, "Drive me to the State Department." "Yes, sir," said the driver, and set off, like Abraham, not knowing whither he went. Seeing an imposing-looking building he drove up, discharged his passenger, and drove rapidly away. The building was the Pentagon, the home of the War Department.

Perhaps he was not so dumb after all! There are many indications that the State Department has been located in the Pentagon. Much of the clutter after World War II resulted from the fact that we were fighting both a political and a military war, and United States attention was too occupied with just a military war. An American general responded to the suggestion that Berlin ought to be occupied before the Russians got there by saying, "I see no strategic advantage to that." There was no military strategy to it. But what a political strategy it would have been! What else but Pentagon thinking explains the obscene spectacle of the United States reaching out to grasp in alliance the bloody hand of Franco? The one thing that can enter the military mind is bases — that is, airplane bases, not bases for future hope in rallying the free peoples of the world to a genuine democratic leadership. They will not rally very enthusiastically to the ally of the worst fascist dictatorship in the world, which is what Spain has been for twenty years.

Herbert Feis contends in his book *The China Tangle* that our primary blunder was the false assumption that China would play a large role in the defeat of

Japan and that therefore *"military considerations out-
weighed all others."* Which they didn't!

Yours,

SIMEON STYLITES.

Do-It-Yourself

Sir: Eternal vigilance is the price of liberty. It is high
time for the tocsin to ring out, calling all husbands to
the defense of the American home. I do not know
what a tocsin is, but I'm ringing it anyhow.

The most vicious and insidious attack on the rights
of American husbands and the peace of the home is the
"do-it-yourself" movement which is sweeping the
country at an appalling rate. The idea is to keep the
head of the house busy every spare moment of the year
making some fool repairs or so-called "improvements"
around the house.

Woodrow Wilson said in immortal words, "The history of freedom is the history of resistance." So here is
a blow for freedom. We need a Resistance Movement!

The whole thing evidently comes from collusion between restless wives, eager to have some sort of chaos
going on, and hardware merchants. It is promoted by
diabolical pictures in the magazines showing agile
steeple jacks putting a new flashing on the chimney or
shingling the roof or making a set of screens, always
with a moronic grin on their faces.

The movement is really moving. The barons of the paint business gleefully announce that in 1953 paint sales gained a hundred million dollars over 1952 and that "the home craftsman is primarily responsible for the increase."

Now cities are starting "do-it-yourself" expositions, at which all sorts of instruments of torture for meditative husbands are displayed. The police ought to suppress them. Propaganda catalogues of homecraft power tools flood the country. Pictures show a birdbrained husband slaving over a circular saw and jointer combination in the cellar, with the wife in the cheering section urging him on. A truer picture would be one showing the oaf falling off the roof or upsetting a bucket of paint on his head.

This is an attack on the fundamental liberties of the key person in our American culture, the head of the house. After a hard day's work at the office or store or baseball park shall we come home to a bombardment of "do-it-yourself" propaganda, with a display of tools and supplies?

You can see what this is doing to the home. Its peace is gone. The loving wife no longer runs and gets the slippers when you get home; she runs and gets the trowel, the paint brush, and the stepladder! It makes for alienation of affections, too. The ideal of American womanhood is no longer the thoughtful, contemplative executive, such as yourself, but some weak-minded Handy Andy who has no more to do than lay cement walks, simonize the car, and paint the garage. When the wife sees one of them she thinks, "I wish I had married one of those!" As though the divorce rate were not high enough as it is!

This movement has gone far enough. If you put in all your time at do-it-yourself pranks, why do it? Perhaps one hope would be to call in the labor unions. I have never been a fan for Mr. Petrillo, but I can see that a czar in the home repair field might do wonders for freedom. Then any worm who allowed himself to be goaded by his wife into a do-it-yourself stunt would have his gas and electricity shut off by sympathetic strikes.

But it is much better in this case to do-it-yourself without benefit of any Petrillo. Just go out in the back yard and practice saying "No!" Strike for your altars and your fires! And make it a sitdown strike! There is a better motto than "do-it-yourself." It is an old one, but good — "Let George do it!"

Yours,

SIMEON STYLITES.

A Show of Hands

Sir: I was in a meeting a few weeks ago when the chairman said, "Let's have a show of hands." Hands went up — quite a showing. Some were clean, some were dirty, some were neutral. I looked at some of the hands and thought, "What wonderful hands for a pickpocket!" Then the thought seized me, "Perhaps they *are* pickpockets!" For these are jittery days. Then I was calmed by a less hysterical reflection on what a marvelous instrument the human hand is.

Then my mind, over which I have little control, slid off the track onto a siding, where it bumped into what, at a hasty glance, looked like an idea. No doubt the glance was too hasty. But here it is.

In these days of gathering gloom, there are four things you can do with your hands.

1. You can wring them. Our country and world are full of hand-wringers these days. There are hosts of people who take their stand beside a Wailing Wall and moan, "Isn't it awful? Alas, alas! The world is going to the dogs. Woe is me!" (Business of wringing hands.) Of course, it *is* awful. The world is poised on the edge of a cliff. But just wringing one's hands over a situation has never accomplished anything but paralysis in all the millenniums since history began.

2. You can fold your hands. That is easy — that is why so many people are doing it. What do they care about what happens to the world? They are having their "quiet time." They are relaxing. They fold their hands over generously proportioned stomachs and go into a coma.

3. You can put your hands in your pockets. Clench your fists and jam them down tight, so that not even a wayward nickel or a venturesome penny can escape. This will add to your security. It will save you from the temptation of some prodigal moment to give some-

thing to some cause. In days of inflation the difficulties
of every organization in the country that depends on
voluntary contributions will be greatly increased —
every social organization and community chest, every
church. But with your hands in your pockets in a
death grip, you don't need to worry. You are safe and
secure.

4. You can lay your hands on some task. The "laying on of hands" has had a large place in Christian history. An ordination with the laying on of hands is always impressive, whether they be those of cardinal,
archbishop, minister, or layman. But the most important laying on of hands ever done happens when a
person lays his hands on a job that needs doing and
does it. I hear that there are plenty of jobs waiting.

Yours,

SIMEON STYLITES.

Permission To Shriek

Sir: Ambitions differ. Some men have been stirred by
majestic ambitions which make the rest of us look
puny. The boy for my money was Gelett Burgess, who
confessed to an unfulfilled ambition to throw an egg
into an electric fan. There was a man with imagination! I have never aspired so high, but I have cherished
for years the ambition to shriek loud and long in a
public meeting, either in church or almost any meet-

ing except a funeral. Perhaps I should have lived back in the days of the "shouting Methodist." (I wonder if that term is just a myth. How long since the "shouting Methodist" became extinct, like the dodo? Fifty years?)

At any rate I pass on to others who have more courage than I my official permission to shriek in meeting for a good cause. Send ten cents to cover mailing costs, and I will send you an engraved certificate of permission to yell piercingly on the following occasions:

1. You are hereby permitted to shriek the next time and every time you hear Christianity solemnly endorsed as a "bulwark against communism." It is that, but we get infinitely weary of having religion patronized merely because it is useful as an aid in supporting something else. To make that merely instrumental use of religion is far more damaging than the most virulent atheistic onslaught. Religion thrives on denial; it withers and dies by patronage. Christianity may be a weapon against communism. That is incidental. To rest its case on that reason is too much like recommending the Bible as a useful book — useful to hold a window open or as an aid in solving crossword puzzles or to throw at a howling cat at midnight. It may be all that, but . . . So when a politician or educator or preacher approves Christianity merely or mainly as a help in defending something — democracy or the "American way of life" or anything else — stand up and yell in godly protest.

2. Not so loud for this one, but it is all right to yell

when the minister asks a congregation, "Shall we pray?" As though he were going to take a vote on that burning question! Wouldn't he be surprised if the audience answered his question by saying, "Oh, let's not"? So, why the question?

3. Perhaps even a fainter shriek should be given when the minister calls for mutilating a great hymn by chopping off its head from its body. If a hymn is worth singing at all, it is worth singing, all of it. It is an impertinence to announce, just for the sake of fidgeting around with the hymn, "Let us sing No. 117, 'How Firm a Foundation,' the first and third stanzas." That may leave the congregation going through the deep waters without setting foot on the opposite shore. It might be just as fitting, when that abomination occurs, to show your respect for a great hymn by singing it clear through, no matter what sort of mayhem is advised from the pulpit. But a yell is shorter.

4. Shriek loudly the next time a speaker, like a man at sea grasping a straw, says, "That reminds me . . ." You know he is a liar. Nothing has reminded him of anything. You know he has been combing *Joe Miller's Joke Book* for the past three days. And he nearly always comes up with a wheeze that Noah told in the long rainy evenings in the ark.

Go ahead.

SIMEON STYLITES.

Six Impossible Things before Breakfast

Sir: Remember the White Queen in *Alice in Wonderland*? There was a gal! As a queen she had Cleopatra, Catherine the Great, and Maria Theresa pushed off the map. She had everything — force, decision, and authority. And she uttered some deathless words. I think of one of them nearly every time I read the newspaper. It is the boasting remark she made to Alice when Alice complained that one of the queen's tall stories was so tall that she couldn't believe it. To which the queen replied, "Nonsense! Take a big breath and you can believe anything. I frequently believe six impossible things before breakfast."

I have no doubt that she did. For, alas, she was not alone in being able to turn that difficult trick. In fact, we seem to have a White Queen civilization, with the world full of people who can and do believe any number of impossible things before breakfast or before lunch or at any time, with or without the aid of a big breath. These impossible things are the illusions about ourselves and our world which are as hard for us to give up as it was for our ancestors to give up the illusion that the earth was flat or that the sun went around the earth. During the last war, a mother whose son was stationed in the Aleutian islands was asked where he was. "I don't know," she answered, "but I think he is in the illusions." That is where a lot of folks live, and here are six of the impossible things they believe:

1. "We can preserve peace by having an armament race." Many people believe that before breakfast. It takes a big breath, but they can manage it. Just get guns and bombs enough and no one will dare fight us. That is what the Original Cave Man said as he fondled a five-foot stone club. "This is the biggest. No one will dare attack me." (Those were his last words, for just then he was beaned from behind.) Arms never prevented a war, but hope springs eternal in the military mind.

2. The fallacy of the Firing Squad. This is the devil theory of history: just kill the devil and things will be O.K. So, many people shouted, "Hang the Kaiser," "Shoot Hitler." The Kaiser and Hitler have passed on. But many folks still believe that if enough people — the right people, of course — are stood up before a firing squad, all our troubles will be over.

3. "We can get a state so perfect that no one will have to be good." (That is a rough paraphrase of T. S. Eliot's sarcasm.) This is a beloved illusion. All the trouble is with outward conditions. Fix them up a bit and there will be no need for any bothersome inner discipline.

4. Modernity is a guarantee of superiority. That sounds silly, but many stout souls can gulp hard and believe it. All you need to do is look at the date. If it is 1950 or so, it is "the best." *From Here to Eternity* is a

greater novel than *Moby Dick;* Ogden Nash is a greater poet than Milton.

5. The permanency of present things. This illusion is a popular before-breakfast diet. Hitler boasted that his Reich would last a thousand years; it did not last a thousand days after the timetable was announced. Yet many people believe that the colonial system will go on, and like little Joshuas they command the sun to stand still.

6. There must be another one. Oh, yes. We see a lot of it in presidential campaigns. It is the illusion that social problems can be settled by incantation. No one would try to fix a leak in the radiator by marching around it seven times and shouting "Abracadabra," but we do it in politics all the time.

Now, let's go to breakfast!

SIMEON STYLITES.

Western Union Theology

Sir: Standing one day at the telegraph counter I was weary and ill at ease, and my fingers wandered idly over the well worn telegraph blanks in the rack on the counter. You know the sort — texts of standardized messages, of which you can just check those to be sent and thus save time by not having to write them out or use any brain sweat thinking what to say. They are for all occasions — births, weddings, graduation, everything except divorce, and the forms for congratulation on divorce will doubtless be along next year. Behold another of the wonders of modern progress!

I noticed a list of canned messages for Easter. Conventional greetings. Check your favorite. What was new to me was a special list of "Bunnykins" for children. I counted them over one by one. The whole assortment seemed not much above the level of "Bunnykins." Here are three top-level samples: "Easter greetings across the miles. Here's wishing you a day of smiles." "Here's hello from your Easter Bunny. May your day be happy, bright and sunny." (Who wouldn't swoon for joy at getting that?) "From far away I wire to say, A very happy Easter Day." (Sounds like Tennyson.)

I was struck by the fact that not one message in the whole list of thirty conveyed the slightest idea of what Easter is all about. Not one. Easter was watered down until it was merely a carnival for the telegraph company. Now, of course, why shouldn't there be forms for sending best wishes for Easter, done up in the most glamorous adjectives? It's a natural thing, a convenience. No need to have an outline of Christian theology. Granted. Still, the wonder comes whether this is not a visible symbol of the growing secularization of Christian holy days, the degradation of holy days into holidays, in which the original meaning is completely submerged. Surely there might be at least one message which could dimly suggest that Easter is the high festival of an articulate Christian faith!

It is a disturbing thought that this Western Union theology is the one accepted by multitudes. Anything definite is blurred; the objective truth and event are blotted out by subjective feeling. Not the lilting affirmation, "Christ is risen," but a sentimental gurgle, "I hope you're feeling happy." This sort of theology forgets that Christianity did not come into the hard Roman world with a fixed grin and a purring "Best wishes, everybody! Hope you are happy!" It was a news broadcast. Something had happened: "Now is Christ risen from the dead."

This drifting fog of silly sentimentality is creating its own ritual and hymns. To multitudes the chief, often the only, Easter hymn is:

> *You'll be the finest lady*
> *In the Easter parade.*

All hail to Western Union, an indispensable boon to our life. But here's hoping it does not become our only source of theology.

Yours,

SIMEON STYLITES.

A Speech for Any Occasion

Sir: A man I used to know fairly well once said that every man should carry about with him two things where he could get at them in a hurry: a reason for the faith that is in him, and a carefully prepared extemporaneous speech which would be fit for any occasion —a wedding, a funeral, or the annual convention of the Elks.

It seems like a good idea. I can't do anything for you about the first; you will have to make your own reason. But I can send you, as a belated New Year's gift, a portable, collapsible speech that will come unrolled in the sight and hearing of any audience, and will get you a reputation as the greatest orator the Loop has produced since Mayor Thompson.

This trick speech, tailored to fit any occasion, is the work of A. Parker Nevin of Princeton University. Mr. Job E. Hedges, who was no mean hurler of after-dinner verbiage, said of it, "You can call it 'The Crisis,' 'Justice,' 'Solution,' 'Destiny,' or anything you want to. It covers the whole range of human thought and is unanswerable." Here goes, then: *

MR. CHAIRMAN, LADIES AND GENTLEMEN:

It is indeed a great and undeserved privilege to address such an audience as I see before me. At no previous time in the history of human civilization have greater problems confronted and challenged the ingenuity of man's intellect than now. Let us look around us. What do we see on the horizon? What forces are at work? Whither are we drifting? Under what mist of clouds does the future stand obscured?

* Reprinted by permission of the Princeton Alumni Weekly.

My friends, casting aside the raiment of all human speech, the crucial test for the solution of these intricate problems to which I have just alluded is the sheer and forceful application of those immutable laws which down the corridors of Time have always guided the hand of man, groping, as it were, for some faint beacon light for his hopes and aspirations. Without these great vital principles we are but puppets responding to whim and fancy, failing entirely to grasp the hidden meaning of it all. We must readdress ourselves to these questions which press for answer and solution. The issues cannot be avoided. There they stand. It is upon you, and you, and yet even upon me, that the yoke of responsibility falls.

What, then, is our duty? Shall we continue to drift? No! With all the emphasis of my being I hurl back the message *No!* Drifting must stop. We must press onward and upward toward the ultimate goal to which all must aspire.

But I cannot conclude my remarks, my dear friends, without touching briefly upon a subject which I know is steeped in your very consciousness. I refer to that spirit that gleams from the eyes of a new-born babe, that animates the toiling masses, that sways all the hosts of humanity past and present. Without this energizing principle all commerce, trade and industry are hushed and will perish from this earth as surely as the crimson sunset follows the golden sunrise.

Mark you, I do not seek to unduly alarm or distress the mothers, fathers, sons and daughters gathered before me in this vast assemblage, but I would indeed be recreant to a high resolve which I made as a youth if I did not at this time and in this place, and with the full realizing sense of responsibility which I assume, publicly declare and affirm my dedication and my consecration to the eternal principles and precepts of simple, ordinary, commonplace *justice*.

You may doubt the magic of this appeal, but I am willing to bet my shirt (Christmas present, $3.95) that it would stir the listeners at a National Undertakers' Convention, the American Legion, or the hundredth anniversary of First Church, to say nothing of the Floor of Congress in a debate either on Red China or a rollback on prices.

Yours,

SIMEON STYLITES.

His Bite Is Worse than His Bark

Sir: "Don't pay any attention to George," she said, apologizing for her husband, who had been growling ferociously in a corner. "His bark is worse than his bite." Listening to that one for the ten thousandth time I thought, "What a wonderful thing it would be to meet someone sometime whose bite is worse than his bark!" I might get bitten, but it would be an exciting change!

What an amazing tribute it would be to a public speaker or a political figure (that is, a figure other than zero) to have it said of him, "His bite is worse than his bark." But alas, that doesn't come much oftener than Halley's Comet. So many orators take it out in barking. It is so easy to bark. That is why so many meetings on public questions, with a long list of speakers, are like the aquarium at feeding time, with a barking of seals that almost raises the roof. It would be a lovely change to meet a mild-mannered man, with a bark no louder than that of a shy and gentle Pekingese, but who bites without much or any barking and sinks his teeth into a specific action.

The main trouble with barking — worse than the din — is that if one barks ferociously enough it brings on the delusion that one has actually done something about the matter. That is the danger of many high-sounding resolutions at church gatherings. There are so many resounding barks and so few real bites. The formula is something like this:

> *Whereas,* the denial of civil rights to any citizen of the United States on account of race or color, is a betrayal of the fundamental principles of democracy; and
>
> *Whereas,* such denials of democracy are the

worst handicap to our nation in its international relations, particularly with Asia and Africa;

    Therefore, be it resolved . . . that we appoint a committee to study the subject and report next year. [End of Bark.]

    Let us adjourn.

Wouldn't it be nice to trade a hundred ferocious barks for one little bite, on actual sinking of the teeth into some concrete situation?

Yours,

SIMEON STYLITES.

The Art of Coming In

Sir: A few years ago Gerald W. Johnson made an injured complaint that the great composers haven't done right by the flute players. He was moved to tears and anger that the great ones provide a score full of vast empty places for the flute. The violins can keep going right along, but the flutist must wait fifteen minutes to play one note. In his own words (from *A Little Night Music*):

> The man who can rest for seventy-four measures, as this man Haydn expects the flutes to do in one place, and then come in correctly on the upbeat of the seventy-fifth, is a man of high and

estimable qualities . . . In the first place, he who can do it has learned to concentrate. In the second place, he has developed mental tenacity, for seventy-four measures last a long time. In the third place, he has mental precision, or he will never come in on the last beat. Finally, he not only has to come in, but he must come in *forte;* that demands self-confidence.

Mr. Johnson calls that "the art of coming in." It is a good one to practice, for most of us are "flutists"; we are not cast for the aria or any big solo part; we just "come in."

Of course, one of the fine parts of this art of coming in is to know when to stay out. That goes particularly for parents. When the youngsters are making their first stabs on their own, just remember that there isn't any music here for you to play. Pipe down. Lay aside the big tuba that you like so well. Don't blow a blast on it. Don't even toot on the piccolo. This goes double when the kids get married. Don't make them, by your untimely music, sigh, "I should have married an orphan."

It is an exciting game to play, just to listen, in our personal relations, for a cue for our coming in with one note. Not like a roaring gust, but like a quiet tide that lifts. It was a wise man, for instance, who gave this advice: "When you have a friend who takes a new job, don't write him a note of congratulation when he is elected. Wait till he has been on the job three months.

By that time all the 'outs' will appear, and he will be wondering what kind of fool he was to take it. That is the time to come in with a note of encouragement." That is not cynicism, but just realism, and it goes for any job. We know a bishop who, after four months in office, was debating between cyanide of potassium and the river.

Dean Charles R. Brown had a lovely imagination by which he picked up the cues for coming in. He showed it in making calls Christmas morning on the families in the parish where a death had occurred during the year. He knew what a hard day Christmas would be. He did not need to say anything; he just came in. So also in another practice. His imagination told him that the hardest moment after a death was not at the funeral service or at the grave. It was coming back to the empty house. That was when he came in!

In political life, too, we must keep an ear cocked for the cue to come in. The loudest cue, at present, is the well-advertised onslaught now preparing by the "un-American activities" boys, on education in the United States. It threatens to be the nearest approach to a Hitler book-burning and Russian "thought control" ever staged in this country. College presidents and school superintendents cannot resist it alone. At a rough guess, it calls for fifty million of us to come in.

So get out your flute. Or better, make ready for a bang on the cymbals.

> Yours,
>
> SIMEON STYLITES.

The Art of Doing Nothing

Sir: I have always been interested in my namesake, the first Simeon Stylites. He was the original flagpole-sitter — and sat there thirty-three years. That is still a world's record. He must also have the record as a columnist, for no one else ever had a column for that length of time.

But it has been hard to find any good about Simeon, other than a vague, undefined saintliness. The soap manufacturers, I am sure, would pay him no honor; he was not lavish with their product. Then, too, there are rumors that his remoteness from it all was a pose. He had quite a flair for floating down directions to people below.

But an essay by George Lamb in *Saints for Now* makes clear that St. Simeon was a real genius. He is to be admired, Mr. Lamb writes, for "that terrific talent of his for doing nothing." "There is no finer slap in the eye to the modern world than that," he adds.

There you have it! One of the world's finest things is a "terrific talent for doing nothing." Simeon has a lot to teach.

It is a real art. Many people think they are doing nothing when they are merely doing something trivial, such as fiddling at something, or dawdling, or playing solitaire, or worrying about the work they should be doing. Thus they miss it on both ends. They do not accomplish anything, and they do not enter the Beatific State of Pure Vacancy.

One prerequisite for the true enjoyment of doing nothing is that you must have plenty to do. Obviously, if you have nothing to do, there is no fun at all in doing nothing. The true enjoyment can only be had when one is buried under a mountain of duties, either real or imaginary. Save up your unanswered letters and bills till they are a foot high, look at a calendar of gloriously forgotten engagements, listen to the unanswered telephone, and you can enter the pure Nirvana of Doing Nothing.

If some earnest moralist points the finger of shame at you, you can snap right back at him that people with a terrific talent for doing nothing have been the world's greatest benefactors. It is a myth that necessity was the mother of invention. The man who said that was barking up the wrong family tree. *Laziness* was the mother of invention. Who invented the wheel? Undoubtedly some lout too lazy to push anything. Sitting under a tree, he saw a stone roll downhill, and got an idea for avoiding work. Who invented the sail? Some lazybones too unenergetic to row a boat. That brings us down to the present day. Here is Clarence Bleicher, president of the De Soto division of Chrysler, saying, "Whenever we have a tough job at the plant and our experts can't find an easy way to do it, we put one of our laziest men on it. He'll find an easy way in 48 hours flat. Then we adopt his method." People who "haven't a lazy bone in their body" frequently have a very lazy bone for a head. The "lazybones," while resting, think of better ways of doing things.

We need more practitioners of the art of doing nothing to counterbalance the folks painfully doing the wrong thing. These are the people whom H. G. Wells called the "Gawdsakers," that is, the people who are always saying, "For Gawd's sake, let's do something." There are lots of that brotherhood around and all very vocal. Some of them are in Congress. They are tired of the Korean War. (Who isn't?) So they say, "Let's do something, anything — bomb Manchuria, invade China. That will be something." (It will.) People with a "talent for doing nothing" might turn it into the most terrific *doing* in the world — thinking.

> Yours,
>
> SIMEON STYLITES THE LESS.

The Temperance Society

Sir: Once upon a time there was a beautiful little village in which the usual societies that thrive in such habitats were present. One of the most flourishing was the Temperance Society. It was made up of very nice people, devoted to their society and to the cause of temperance. All of their meetings were marked by impressive displays of moving eloquence and applause.

There was only one small drawback to their work. They were drunk most of the time. Not all the time. They rarely began serious drinking till after lunch. And they were pleasant drunks — humorous, genial, eloquent, but still, alas, drunks. Their small-minded and bigoted neighbors were more impressed by their actions at the tavern than by their eloquence at the meetings of the Temperance Society. They did not make many converts.

Now, if you think that fable fantastic, listen to another, which is, alas, true.

In the same village there was what was known as an "Ecumenical Movement." Practically all church members from the nineteen different Protestant churches were in it. They gathered together to give high praise to church unity. They bowed in earnest prayer, asking forgiveness for the "sin of schism," and made prayers for the unity of all the people of God.

There was only one small drawback to this flourishing movement. All the time they kept working for disunity. In spite of the fervent praying, they all guarded, like a nervous bulldog, every denominational difference. Even on the most minute points of difference, scarcely visible to the naked eye of the bewildered townsmen, they took their stand like Martin Luther, saying, "Here I stand, I can do no other!" It is sad to relate that their small-minded and bigoted neighbors were more impressed by their actions for preserving disunity than by their ecstatic praise of unity. So

the good ship *Ecumenical* was becalmed in the dol-
drums.

In the case of the Temperance Society, it seems that
the alternatives might be to give up drinking or to
give up the Temperance Society. After long study of
the matter, I come out flatly for giving up drinking.

In the case of the village Ecumenical Movement, the
alternatives seem to be to give up the oratory and
prayers for church unity or to do something about
church unity in the village. After long study of the
matter, I come out flatly for doing something about
it.

Yours,

SIMEON STYLITES.

The Voice of Angels

Sir: Did anyone ever tell you that you had "the voice
of an angel"? Probably not. Yet we so often hear the
expression, "He had the voice of an angel," that I got
to wondering what an angel would sound like. So I did
some research. Everyone else is doing it; why not I?
They tell me that there are some colleges which have
more white rats performing experiments than they
have students. I wanted to get a cellarful of white rats
to prove something — I had not yet decided what. But
the family objected. So I went in for research on the

Bible. And I have discovered (this will be a big scoop for *The Christian Century*) what an angel's voice sounds like. I will not keep you in suspense. It sounds remarkably like a person saying, "Hurry up!"

You see, up to the time when I took over, research had been blocked because it was based on the delusion that the voice of an angel would always be "beautiful." The words "Get up" are rarely beautiful, never less so than at seven a.m. Yet that is what the angels always say when they talk to men, as reported in the Bible. Of course, I am not a walking *Strong's Exhaustive Concordance*, but I can't at the moment think of anything an angel ever said but "Get up and hurry!" An angel comes to Peter in jail and says, "Rise quickly." An angel says to Gideon, "Arise and go in this thy might." An angel says to Elijah, "Arise and eat." An angel appears to Joseph in a dream, when Herod was slaughtering the infants, and says, "Go quickly." An angel appears to Philip, in the book of Acts, and says, "Arise and go."

Really, the angels are monotonous talkers! They always say the same thing — "Arise, hurry!" But so is a fire bell monotonous. If we are to be saved it will be by monotony, the reiterated command, "Get up and get going!"

Listen carefully and you can hear the voice of angels above the contemporary din of the world, a voice that ought to get us out of lounge chairs and comfortable beds. "Arise, go quickly!" In the lull that follows after the Japanese peace treaty, there is hurry demanded that we bring to Asia arguments other than a gun barrel, that we bring a magic more potent than the economic and political voodoo and mumbo-jumbo of the Communist witch doctors. Arise and go quickly to Cicero, Illinois, and a thousand other towns.

It might be a good idea to allow an angel to occupy the pulpit in the meetinghouse at 11 a.m. on Sunday. An irate hearer said to Samuel Barnett when he was canon of Bristol Cathedral in England, "I come to church to be comforted, and you sound like a fire alarm." Perhaps there was a fire.

Yours,

SIMEON STYLITES.

If the Founders Came Back

Sir: The night I went to a first performance of Margaret Webster's production of *Saint Joan,* by Bernard Shaw, it was being "tried out on the dog," and I was one of the dogs. I had a lot of fun, yelping and barking with appreciation all over the place. In my canine opinion, the play holds up as well as any of the other hardy perennials.

Once again, the last scene is very provocative. In the midst of all the celebrations in her honor, Saint Joan appears and says in effect, "I did not know you loved me so much. I will come back." And the response: "Horrors, no! Anything but that!"

That scene raises a very interesting and embarrassing question: What if the Founders came back? It brings to mind the observation that prophets are twice stoned — once when they are alive and again when stone monuments are erected over them after they are safely dead. If they came back, perhaps they would be stoned a third time.

Try it on most any institution or organization. If, in the midst of the anniversary honors and genuflections, some of the founders were to come back, and be the same difficult folks they were when alive, the cry of their descendants might well be, "For heaven's sake, crawl back up on your pedestal while we bring some more wreaths!"

This would be a healthy speculation for all organizations of Sons and Daughters, all the professional Descendants. For instance, stage this scene in your imagination:

The national convention of the Daughters of the American Revolution is opening. The hall is filled with blue bloods and red-white-and-blue bloods. After the national anthem, the presiding officer proudly announces, "We have with us today two of the Fathers of the Revolution, Mr. Samuel Adams and Mr. Thomas Paine."

What would happen if old Sam Adams, the rabble-rouser from Massachusetts, in his slovenly clothes, should stalk out on the stage and let go in his usual form about the blessedness of rebellion? Or if Tom Paine were to follow in the strain of the most disrespectful parts of *Common Sense?* Well, here's about what the A.P. dispatch would say:

> WASHINGTON, D.C. — In the midst of Mr. Paine's address at Constitution Hall, 101 delegates fainted. Eighteen ambulances were rushed to the scene. The program committee, which was held responsible for the appearance of these speakers (both on lists of subversives), was severely reprimanded.

If you are feeling strong enough, picture Abraham Lincoln addressing the Republican national convention. Or — let's be nonpartisan — Thomas Jefferson addressing the Democrats.

Or think of the Founding Fathers of various denominations attending the national synod, or an eleven o'clock service on Sunday. They would find a lot to rejoice in, and don't you forget it! But might there not often be lifted eyebrows among the delegates, or in the pews, while they asked, "How did our revolutionary movement ever dwindle down into this Society for the Preservation of Antiquities?" Martin Luther, John Knox, John Wesley, Alexander Campbell — stay away from our door!

Then, of course, you might think of another Founder, come back and, as his custom was, going to the morning service. You can work that one out for yourself.

Yours,

SIMEON STYLITES.

Indianapolis!

Sir: My friends in Indiana (I have three of them and can prove it) may not like this letter, thinking that the story in it disparages the capital of the Valley of Democracy. But it is really a high tribute and I hope they will see it that way.

Time magazine once quoted a remark of Katharine Hepburn, the actress, which deserves a place in many a memory book. She was in the wings of a New York theater, just about to go on the stage in a new play, *The Philadelphia Story,* and was almost congealed with fear. Her previous appearance in New York had been a failure and naturally she was nervous. She said that as she waited for the fatal moment and her cue, she kept saying over and over to herself, "This is Indianapolis! This is Indianapolis!" Apparently, Indianapolis would be less terrifying than New York. It must have worked, for in *The Philadelphia Story* she had one of her greatest successes.

Now when the higher criticism is brought to bear on that incident it is clear that Miss Hepburn was not regarding Indianapolis as a hick town where anything goes. She was just reassuring herself that those white spots out in the audience were not all savage drama critics with daggers ready, but human faces, people, just like the folks in Indianapolis. And, since they were members of the human race, she could say with Shake-speare, "If you tickle us, do we not laugh?" It was a sweetly solemn thought.

It would be a great thing if more public speakers could remember, "This is Indianapolis!" So many get so frozen with fear that they cannot hit the ball at all. This is true of most political oratory. We saw it painfully, and heard it even more painfully, in two conventions last summer. So many of the hoarse key-noters seemed to have told themselves, "This is a great occasion. I must turn on the big bow-wow machine." The result was a ghastly noise. Even the orator's partisans could think of nothing but to batten down the hatches and wait for the big wind to blow over. The orators should have said to themselves, "This is Indianapolis. Strange as it may seem, those things out there are people. Why not talk to them in their native language?"

The same thing is true of the pulpit. The preacher comes up to a "great" occasion and all too often meditates, "I must hit a home run." So he strains to knock one over the fence, with the usual result — a strike-out. The constant bane of the college chapel is the preacher's failure to remember, "This is Indianapolis." He says to himself: "This is a new kind of zoo. All sorts of dangerous animals roam here, professors and heavy intellectuals. This calls for my major opus on 'The Past, Present and Future of Civilization.'" So civilization gets a workout and the audience gets sleeping sickness. The orator should remember that the people in the audience carry union membership cards in the human race, Local 704. Perhaps they came not to hear Spinoza refuted or Barth either applauded or confounded, but to worship. Could be.

On to Indianapolis!

Yours,

SIMEON STYLITES.

Picking Up Your Cap

Sir: Win, lose, or draw, I am still a Brooklyn Dodger fan. The records show that in many respects the Dodgers have never been matched. For instance, years ago they mastered the art of having two men on third base at the same time. In such arts they do not now reach the heights of the old days when they were known as the Daffiness Boys. Whether they won pennants or not, they added to the gaiety of the game. One historical fact deserves recording. It may not stand on the same level with Magna Charta or the battle of Waterloo, but it has its points. An outfielder, "Babe" Herman, rated by many admirers as Zany No. 1, was running to catch a fly ball. His cap was blown off, and as he stopped to pick it up the ball dropped to the ground, and what ought to have been an easy out became a two-base hit.

The picture of "Babe" Herman stopping to pick up his cap often comes to mind. Whenever a person misses the main point of an occasion through devotion to some minor detail or inconsequential misfortune, he is a fielder stopping to pick up his cap when he ought to be catching the ball.

That happens all the time in many homes. When the care of the house displaces in importance the climate of the home, someone has stopped to pick up her cap. She has missed the main point of the home. Come to think of it, that was the main point in the record of the best known dinner scene in all history, when Jesus dined in the home of Mary and Martha. The Guest, in his rebuke to Martha, was not disparaging cooking or table-setting. It was simply that, on that occasion, she missed the main point, which was not food but fellowship for the mind and soul.

Emerson made the same plea somewhere, like this: "I pray you, O excellent wife, do not disturb your soul to set before your guest the perfect meal. He can get that in any inn for a dollar [pre-inflation prices]. But remember that fellowship, the meeting of mind and heart, he cannot get for any price at any inn." (Free translation by Simeon.)

Here is a gal who had the right idea, who never stopped to pick up her cap when big things were going on, Grandma Moses. She had a houseful of children. Being normal they were wild. They ran the bathtub to overflowing and flooded the house. Her sister growled, "If I were you I wouldn't stand it." Grandma replied, "Kids are the big thing in this house. I'd like to give them some good times to remember." She did! Evidently she believed the Man who said it all in five words: "Life is more than meat."

In many directions we can see the fielder with no sense of priority. There is the politician in the midst of the issue of human survival, who stops dead in his tracks to pick up some partisan advantage. There is the teacher intent on picking up a cap with a feather in it — a reputation for minute research, which often becomes mere pedantry — while his real opportunity — to communicate truth with contagious enthusiasm — drops to the ground.

Yours,

SIMEON STYLITES.

Letter to 10,000 Wives

Sir: Will you please see that this letter is delivered to the addressee?

Mrs. A. Homo
Anytown, U.S.A.

DEAR MRS. HOMO: Encumbered as you are these summer days with tending the garden and mowing the lawn, you have probably not had time to notice a far-reaching judicial decision that affects every wife in America, including you. It is a decision which at last asserts the rights of the most oppressed group in America, the Down-Trodden Husbands (not Incorporated).

In brief, a court granted a divorce to the movie actor Franchot Tone from his wife of a few weeks, Barbara Payton, on the grounds that "she embarrassed him before company." Your quick mind will instantly grasp how profoundly this decision affects the whole domestic scene. So watch your step. And, particularly, your lips. There are nine and twenty ways to embarrass your husband, with new ones invented every time a sweet young thing says, "I do." Here are a few now forbidden by the majesty of the law.

1. Don't say, "I've heard that one before, dear." Of all the sad words, those take the prize. A husband's highest pride is always as a raconteur, a teller of tales. To be stopped in full flight in the midst of a masterpiece is an embarrassing deflation. Edwin Booth played Hamlet a thousand times. Why shouldn't your husband recount as often as that the drama of when he put a traffic policeman in his place?

2. Don't interrupt your Master to correct him before company. Don't strike a sour note by exclaiming, "You are wrong, sweetheart! That didn't happen at Santa Monica, California, but at Caribou, Maine. Remember?"

3. Don't reveal publicly that your husband is a liar. Remember that imagination is a divine gift. Don't wither it. Don't break in on a tense climax by exclaiming, "But we were never in Moscow, darling! How could Stalin have been talking to you?"

4. Don't seize the moment when all eyes are on your husband to brush off imaginary lint from his coat, as

though you were a Pullman porter or the mother of a retarded child.

5. Don't apologize for your husband's limitations. When the roast chicken comes onto the dinner table don't say, with a cheerful giggle, "Poor dear Anthropos never learned to carve. The chicken will be off on the floor in a minute, or in your lap. Watch out!" That may add to the gaiety of the party, but it is now grounds for divorce.

6. When your husband goes to sleep in the midst of the lecture, or in the living room while the guest of honor is giving her autobiography *in extenso,* don't wake him up abruptly and ostentatiously, so that his bewilderment becomes a public merriment. Be subtle. Easy does it.

I am not criticizing. I am just giving you the news from the world of law. Govern yourself accordingly.

> Defiantly,
>
> SIMEON STYLITES.

Total Recall

Sir: I do not know who invented the affliction known to psychologists as "total recall" — whether it was Freud, Jung, or merely Mrs. Whosis — but it is really quite something, when you hear it in action. It may not be as dangerous to life as the new brands of virus, so popular this year, but it has twinges of its own. As done in its best form it means exactly what the name says: the ability — and eagerness — to recall everything, which means *everything*.

The commonest variety of sufferer is the person who takes the words of greeting "How are you?" not as a salutation but as an invitation to report on clinical research, and he recalls the total situation of lungs, lights, and liver.

Or take another species. The conversation is moving along — nothing momentous, but it *is* moving — when he is struck with total recall, like a sudden attack of apoplexy. He — in my experience it is usually she — tunes up. Someone has unfortunately mentioned Los Angeles. That does it! The total recall is on. Her visit to the place is unrolled all the way from the "unusual" rain to the plots, if any, of all the broadcasts to which she got free tickets, including the biography of the man who gave the tickets, who turned out, this will kill you, to be a nephew of Minnie Wilkins, you know, who used to teach school at Seneca Falls, N.Y. It is the nearest thing to perpetual motion yet devised.

A special case, or an aggravated one, is a wife's total recall. That puts the husband on the hot seat for an hour or so. Something snaps, and the loving wife goes into a complete remembrance of every bonehead act poor Jim ever pulled off, beginning with the forgotten railroad tickets on the wedding journey, and coming up by uneasy stages to the time he got arrested for telling off a traffic policeman, with a detour ten minutes) about the upset canoe. This makes poor Jim, who is thus portrayed as a candidate for a mental hospital, think longingly of the fine old judicial decision of English law that it was permitted to hit your wife with a "reasonable instrument." (Is a nice soft towel, soaked with chloroform, a "reasonable instrument"?)

Total recall, on the platform or in the pulpit, is the world's best cure for insomnia. Robert Louis Stevenson said that if he knew how to omit he could make an *Iliad* out of a daily newspaper. The total recallers can create a 48-page Sunday supplement out of an obscure footnote. There is so much detail in the background that the foreground goes underground.

What can be done about it? Nothing, I suppose, except resignation to the will of God. However, here is a four-point program to work on:

1. Try to forget one thing a day. That is slow, but concentrate! There is the time you had to walk down the Eiffel Tower. It is a gorgeous conversation piece, like one of the old Paine's fireworks. Forget it!

2. Try tying up your jaws with an old stocking. Do it by degrees, five minutes at first, then up to an hour. Practice makes perfect.

3. Give your ears, instead of your jaws, a workout for a change.

4. Enroll in a memory course. That will paralyze your memory, trying to remember the clue techniques.

I can't recall anything else.

                                   Yours,

                                          SIMEON STYLITES.

Thirty Pieces of Silver

Sir: Whatever became of the thirty pieces of silver paid to Judas for the betrayal of Jesus? The Lenten season brings to mind the endlessly attractive speculations about what happened to the physical properties in the story of the crucifixion. Lloyd Douglas traced in his novel *The Robe* what might have been the later history of Jesus' seamless garment. Walter Rauschenbusch made a searching study of the subsequent history of Pilate's washbowl, reaching the disturbing conclusion that we have all used it in an attempt to escape responsibility.

Judas' thirty pieces of silver have likewise engaged the imagination of men, particularly in the Middle Ages — though many writers have been more concerned with where the thirty pieces came from than with where they went to. In the twelfth century Godfrey of Viterbo, in his *Pantheon,* wrote that one of the first appearances of these famous coins was when they were paid to Joseph's brothers for Joseph. One ingenious writer, with a lively imagination, asserted that the executioners of the Apostle Paul in Rome were paid with the thirty pieces, and that the identical coins were used again to reward the men who burned Joan of Arc. So we might imagine that the price of all dark betrayals was the same handful of silver, all the way from Benedict Arnold to Klaus Fuchs.

Where do we come in? Don't worry, we come in all right! Loose the checkrein of your imagination on the subject and it will pull up at some surprising and embarrassing places. Any kind of betrayal of duty is paid in full with one or more of the pieces of silver given to Judas.

Often that betrayal is nothing more dramatic than spending all our silver on ourselves. If we listen carefully we can hear the clink of Judas' coins hitting each other when we spend all of what might have been a part of the world's capital for welfare on ourselves in the form of immediate, personal dividends. Dick Sheppard had a better idea. He wrote, "I am often strapped for personal funds, but I always have charitable money."

Often the thirty pieces of Judas' silver have turned up in payment to people just for keeping still. More of the silver with the dark history has been paid for keeping still than for speaking out. Keeping still is easier. Some raw deal is being railroaded through. We know it. But we are busy. Besides, why should we stick our necks out? Clink! Clink! There are lots of people whose necks seem to be the most important part of them. These neck preservers do not do the dirty work themselves. They just stand by, consenting, sometimes holding the clothes of those who stone Stephen.

The thirty pieces of silver have grown to millions. They are paid out each year for services, big or little, to the devil. Every bonus that is paid in the form of prestige, position, or advantage for services rendered to exploiting gangs is Judas money. The check may pass through the clearinghouse, but it is silver just the same. Listen — clink!

> *Still as of old*
> *Men by themselves are priced —*
> *For thirty pieces Judas sold*
> *Himself, not Christ.*

Yours,

SIMEON STYLITES.

Bluebeard — American Version

Sir: One of the best-remembered joys of the childhood of many people, including yours respectfully, is the gory murders of the story of Bluebeard. I hope no psychological tenderness — which I view with alarm — will be allowed to deprive the coming generations of children of their needed quota of blood and thunder as supplied by the Brothers Grimm and the *Arabian Nights*. If the excitements of violence and murder most foul are replaced by the placidities of *The Bobbsey Twins at Camp,* we will have a race of degenerates on our hands. Bluebeard was tops. Seven bodies in one closet! Or was it only five?

Reveling in such memories, I got to thinking that there is another version of the Bluebeard story, what might be called an American Version. Not the story of an inner room concealing wicked crimes, but a true story of the inner room of the mind and soul in which there is — nothing at all! Not the tragedy of homicide, but the tragedy of a vacuum.

For if the inmost room of the soul could be broken open, that is what would be found in many present-day Bluebeards — nothing.

It was only the other day the newspapers reported the case of a man in Cincinnati who had been nine years in a coma. He is not alone. There are plenty of folks who have been in a spiritual and intellectual coma for more than nine years. Their secret room holds a terrible secret — it is stark empty. That accounts for the very great popularity of the many gadgets for killing time. That seems to be the only use for time — kill it! And the tools of murder multiply daily, waging war on solitude, meditation, and reading. H. G. Wells wrote truly that "people can go through life fudging, evading and sidestepping till their first contact with elemental realities is the cold sweat of their deathbed." Indeed one wonders whether the reason many people fear dying so much is that it is the first thing in all their lives that they ever do alone.

Hawthorne touched on this sad theme in his story "Feathertop," that admired and envied figure in a New England town. He was a glittering figure, yet there seemed to be something not quite right about him. When he was run over by a carriage it was discovered that he was filled with sawdust.

The American Bluebeard has many equivalents for sawdust to disguise the vacuum. A radio manufacturer pointed to one in a large advertisement some time ago, a picture of a family looking at a radio with ecstatic joy, and underneath the words, "Our fondest memory — the day our Magna Vox came!" Rather a thin life for Mr. and Mrs. Bluebeard and little Susie and Bobbie Bluebeard when the fondest memory could be any box or vox. Jack Gould steps into the living room and reports on the vacuum filled with a television set: "The family's evening is not tainted with such an archaic pursuit as conversation. A mute tranquility has overtaken the American home." Stephen Spender has given a transatlantic view: *

> . . . these bald at thirty Englishmen
> Whose polished foreheads are
> The tombs of record sales.

I am glad that my space is more than exhausted, so that no one can ask me about a cure for the vacuum. What would you suggest? Please wire (not collect) to

Yours,

SIMEON STYLITES.

Is There a Doctor in the House?

Sir: The well-known question above has often been repeated in anxious tones from the stage of theater and concert hall. We deeply regret to report that a fre-

* From *Poems* by Stephen Spender, reprinted by permission of the publisher Random House, Inc.

quent, all too frequent, answer to that question today is, "No, the doctor is in the office."

Perhaps we are suffering from an inflamed case of nostalgia. But even so, we do sing fervently and often, "Backward, turn backward, O Time, in your flight," to the good old days when, if you were sick, you could send for the doctor and have him come to the house. Yes, that is what we said, come to the *house*! There *was* a doctor in the house back in the Golden Age. Now, when you are sick, you usually have to hobble down to the doctor's office and wait for an hour and a half and read the *National Geographic Magazine* for June 1941.

Of course, we know that the fine breed of Noble Romans of the medical profession is not extinct. There is still a shining army of martyrs who will go to a house to see a patient. But with the galloping age of specialization, more and more the best you get is a cordial, "Come down to the office." Your wife calls up excitedly: "George has a fever of 105 degrees and cannot breathe, and in addition to that he has just fallen down the cellar stairs and broken both his legs. Can you come over?" The reply comes in dulcet tones, "Have him come down to the office tomorrow."

Thank you! Or is it Thank you?

You see, I am low in my mind. And undoubtedly unfair and ignorant. But I'm getting nervous. I notice that the G.A.R. is reduced to a total strength of one man, or is it two? I am afraid that the time may come when the Grand Army of Family Physicians will be reduced to one doctor, a quaint survival who will, on request, go out to the barn and hitch up the car and come out to see you in your *house*.

And think what the kids are missing in the way of a liberal education! Is there any reader old enough to remember the excitement of having a doctor in the house, with the deep mysteries of the black bag, and the reassurance that all the little bottles of pills gave to everyone, and the acquaintance and friendship which laid the foundation of the doctor's knowledge of each member of the family as an individual person, and not merely as an impersonal assemblage of symptoms?

Yours,

SIMEON STYLITES.

Anoint the Elbows

Sir: I did not get to the coronation of Queen Elizabeth. I had to stay home and cut the grass. I sent my regrets. I approved of it, and if I could have got tickets to Westminster Abbey I would have mortgaged the house and gone.

I did read about it, though, and one thing that sticks in my memory is the story someone dug up of Samuel Pepys's report of the coronation of Charles II. Evidently back in 1660 the anointing was a real full-size ceremony and no little token affair. For the king stripped to the waist and was plentifully anointed on the head, the chest, the shoulders, the back, and the *elbows*! It was the elbows that got my attention. The idea of anointing the elbow is a good one. What is the use of an anointed head and heart if the elbows have not been oiled, so that they can get into motion and do a job?

To be sure, the anointing of the elbow did not "take" with Charles. He was never much on flexing an elbow on a job of work. The familiar couplet about him might well serve as an epitaph —

> *He never said a foolish thing*
> *And never did a wise one.*

The doing was minus.

Poor Charles II was not the only mortal to be weak in the elbow. There are many. It is a common complaint, though the complaining is done by other folks they let down. Quite a company of folks should have their elbows anointed. Their heads are clear, their hearts are "in the right place," but they have arthritis in the elbow. They cannot, or will not, reach down to lift anything. In that respect they are not fully anointed for any work, any more than many of the savage warriors of the Franks were fully baptized.

You remember that among the Franks whole armies were sometimes given baptism at one stroke, and many warriors went into the water with their right hands held high, so that they did not get wet. Then they could say, "This hand has never been baptized," and they could swing their battle axes just as freely as ever. The modern counterpart of that partial baptism is seen in the many people who have been baptized, all except their pocketbooks. They hold those high out of the water.

There is a common phrase of disdain, "He can't tell his head from his elbow," which has real and exact meaning. That is what ails many people — they cannot tell their head from their elbow, cannot tell the difference between an idea in the head only and an idea in the elbow. Their ideas are usually good, but they never think of backing them up with the elbow of action. Thus many people can talk earnestly for an hour on what is wrong with the City Council, but have no anointed elbows to do anything to improve the political life of the city. Some can lecture learnedly on what is wrong with the public schools, but have no oil in the elbows that would enable them to work to improve the schools. Some can see the idiocy of Senator Knowland's grandiose invasion of China, but will not do any real work for the preservation of national sanity.

Yours,

SIMEON STYLITES.

Apparition at a Board Meeting

Sir: A literary critic once adduced as evidence that the
poet William Butler Yeats was a mystic, given to seeing ghosts and other out-of-bounds appearances, the
fact that he once saw an apparition at a board meeting
— a meeting of the Board of Directors of the Abbey
theater in Dublin.

Rather a fascinating idea, an apparition at a board
meeting. For such a meeting is usually the last place
where a ghost or an ethereal wraith or an apparition
would be expected. In many boards the only apparition that appears is the figure of the sheriff, just one
jump behind the bank balance, armed with the papers
to close out the whole works. But he is too real and
substantial to be a ghost.

It might be a good thing if more boards of various
sorts were disturbed at their agenda by unscheduled
appearances of ghosts. Sir William Orpen, the British
artist, after the close of the First World War painted
a picture of an apparition which, alas, was never clearly
seen. It was a painting of the Paris Peace Conference
of 1919, with foreign ministers cutting up maps and
dividing the loot, and the ghost of a soldier, wounded
and bandaged, coming into the room. Clearly the
soldiers did not qualify as a delegate and no one paid

any attention to him. The apparition of a dead soldier ought to be highly visible at every diplomatic conference.

We can think of many Board of Directors' meetings at which an uninvited apparition would be all to the good. Some of the big companies that stride the earth like a Colossus, for instance. Suppose, just before a melon is cut up into dividends, a vision of the consumer, perplexed and haggard, should appear. A chair ought to be set for him.

Try this over on your imagination. The Board of Trustees of First Church is in session. The property committee has reported everything in good order. The finance committee has noted some successful "conversions." Happy thought! But it appears that the "conversions" were of 3 per cent bonds into 4 per cents. Then an apparition appears which all can see. The figure of a Carpenter comes in, the doors being shut, and takes a seat in the rear and listens. Finally he asks two old questions, reported elsewhere: "What is this conversation which you are holding with each other?" and "What were you discussing by the way?" Those might be embarrassing, but they are the number one questions for any church board.

Another apparition might well be an Unseen Client of the church, one of the millions of the least and the last, like those the prophet Micah saw — "the pinched faces of starved peasants peering through the fences."

If you know any member of the official board of a

church, you might get him to read this at the October
meeting.

Yours,

SIMEON STYLITES.

Taking Off the Scum

Sir: Justice Oliver Wendell Holmes, in a letter to Harold Laski, paid high tribute to the power of paradox.
He wrote: "Paradox takes the scum off the mind."

Certainly anything that takes the "scum" off the
mind is a boon to humanity. There are great glories in
the human mind — "how noble in reason, how infinite
in faculty." But there is one "out" about it: it can get
rapidly covered with scum. It can be overlaid with
stagnant deposits if there are no strong currents and
motions to wash them away. The scum may even solidify. Christopher Morley warned against that calamity when he said, "Take your mind out and dance on
it. It is getting all caked up."

The dictionary says that a paradox is "a statement
or proposition seemingly self-contradictory or absurd,
yet explicable as expressing a truth." Thus it may give
the mind a bad jolt, which induces circulation. An
unfamiliar statement may act as a sudden squall on
the dead calm of the mind, and thus take off the scum.
The master of paradox, Jesus, encountered lots of
scum in the minds of men, deposits made by long and

unexamined tradition. A paradox such as "he that loseth his life shall find it" blew away a lot of scum, even though it left waves of anger in many minds. Jesus brought to minds the sacrament of disturbance. It was painful but beneficial.

Of course, too much paradox may be as bad as too much of anything else. Turning out paradoxes is often a form of exhibitionism, like a child on a bicycle calling excitedly, "Look, mom, no hands!" Inordinate addiction to paradox was Mr. Chesterton's trouble. As someone said, trying to look at a serious theme with him was like trying to view the landscape with the aid of a boy's fireworks; the occasional rocket was notable in itself, but the intervening squibs were numerous and distracting. Yet it is true that standing a truth on its head, upside down, often agitates the scum. It compels thinking.

Contradiction too can take the scum off the mind. A sharp, vigorous contradiction of what one has held as an axiom has the effect of a blow on the head — not the kind that puts you to sleep but the kind that wakes you up. A contradiction may act like the gong at the beginning of a round in a prize fight; it brings the person contradicted into the center of the ring in fighting trim. A great host of people, in their reading, for instance, have too much sweet and complacent "Amen" and not enough irritant causing them to cry out, "Is that so?" A reading list for preachers that is greatly needed is one naming a dozen of the most unmannerly, nasty denials of all they hold dear. That

would put adrenalin into the mind and flex the muscles of the brain.

Strangely enough, putting a truth into plain, vigorous English, colloquial talk clear as sunlight, can bring
a terrific shock to a sleepy mind and work havoc with
the scum gathered on it. Much formal utterance has
no more effect on the higher brain centers than the
rumble of a truck going by outside. Someone has said
that a sentence like this: "The sociological utility of
the indeterminate jail sentence has long been recognized," does not disturb sleep at all. But if it is put
this way: "Jones should go to jail and Brown should
say when he comes out," you will discover, with a
thrill of horror, that you have to think. Horrible, but
rough on the scum!

Yours,

SIMEON STYLITES.

'By the Dawn's Early Light'

Sir: Mr. Emerson once wrote a piece called "Compensation." I know that, for I had to read it in school. Like
everything else I read in school, I have forgotten it.
Yet I have a dim idea of what it was about. The main
point seemed to be that "what you lose on the round-
abouts, you make up on the swings," as the English
song has it.

Now I have a little footnote to Mr. Emerson's thesis.

There are real compensations to some terrible things. Item, there are even some compensations to the ghastly experience of having to get off a train at 5 a.m. That is a rude awakening, to scramble out of your Pullman berth and face the hard reality of a railroad station, as gay as a mausoleum, with alert nose, trying to catch the whiff of a cup of coffee. (Detour: Bless the saints who brew coffee at 5 a.m. The Lord make his face to shine upon them!)

But even coffee is a small compensation compared to other things at that hour. By the dawn's early light you can see and feel a reality of fellowship between people who have to be on the job at that grim hour which surpasses much that usually goes under that word. "Fellowship" is usually a high-brow, literary, ten-dollar word. It goes well in sermons and improving books, but you hardly expect to meet it at a lunch counter. But you do meet it early in the morning, and it is the real thing. You get it in the trainman's greeting to the cleaning woman, pushing a mop: "Hi, Maggie," and in her reply: "Howya, Bill." There is no condescension there. There is respect for the job to be done and for the person doing it. You hear and feel it at the lunch counter, where the dawn patrol of labor lingers for a moment. Under the banter and razzing and volleys of genial insult there is a very evident foundation of respect and a feeling of "togetherness." It is no joke to be stirring at dawn, and the people who do it seem conscious of belonging to a fraternal order — in fact to the greatest of them all, the human race, the clan of people who do a job. If one wanted to get lyrical one could paraphrase Isaiah's great passage:

The craftsman encourages the goldsmith,
  and he who smooths with the hammer him who
    strikes the anvil,
saying of the soldering, "It is good."
Every one helps his neighbor,
  and says to his brother, "Take courage!"

So we might say of the railroad station: "The switch-man encourages the scrubwoman and the waitress encourages the Red Cap." They are maintenance people who hold the fabric of the world together, and the job is a strong bond between them.

Perhaps there is a universal law here, of the sort that Toynbee likes to discover every few pages. Try it anyhow. Fellowship that is more than a nice word is always built around some kind of work, among people who are doing a job. Whenever people say, "Go to now, let's have fellowship, just in itself!" the result is a sorry fizzle. Who knows, perhaps there might be more fellowship in the churches, of the sort that still pulses in the pages of the New Testament, if there were more people working on a job. For, as Henry Ward Beecher observed nearly a century ago, "we are called, not only to sit together in heavenly places, but to stand together in unheavenly places."

Yours,

SIMEON STYLITES.

'Klunk!'

Sir: If Lord Dunsany were not already a Lord he should have been knighted for a few warm words he exploded not long ago in London. He was paying his respects, if that is the proper word, to the pretentious lunatic fringe of ultramodern poetry. He was not afraid of being called by that nasty name, "traditionalist." He admitted that our age may be chaotic but, he added, "it does not want chaotic messages. If you are lost in a fog, you do not want a foggy answer."

But what we are giving him a laurel crown for here is his gift of an expressive word, "klunk." He said that many modern poems are bells of lead; "they should tinkle melodiously, but usually they just klunk."

A grand word for speeches; they do go "klunk." Listen and you can hear them now! A mettalic thud indicating that all is lost. At the last annual meeting of the P.T.A., Simeon made a speech that was a komplete klunk.

What makes a speech go "klunk"?

Sometimes it is language. No gritty detail, which, like sand on a slippery road up a hill, will give traction for the mind. There are speakers who talk like this:

. . . regardless of their pigmentation or coloration under normal illumination, felines of all species, it has been learned authoritatively, have been found to be cinereous when the earth becomes enveloped in tenebrosity.

What they mean is "All cats are gray at night." But they would lose caste if they said it that way.

This may sound exaggerated, but if it does you have not heard as many sermons on Existentialism as I have.

Now, behold, I show you a mystery. Why is it that so many speeches and sermons on Ecumenicity and the Ecumenical Church go "klunk!" and become as soporific as laudanum? It is the most wonderful subject in the world, but it will sink most any oratorical craft.

We have known magnificent speakers, who ordinarily move with all the agility and deadly effectiveness of a destroyer. But when they take the subject of Ecumenicity, they give a gurgle and the ship goes down forty fathoms deep. The reason is, in large part, that there is no detail, nothing for the eye to follow, all a struggle for definition and talk of generalities.

Many speeches go "klunk!" because of a lack of narrative. That is part of the unfailing power of the parables of Jesus. Narrative has kept Aesop very much alive for many centuries. Take that most gifted speaker of all times, the Ancient Mariner. Notice how he begins a speech: "There was a ship, quoth he." That gave him a half-nelson on his audience. He did not begin, "Now let us consider the principles of navigation." He knew a trick worth two of that. He held his audience by narrative. Look at the record:

> *He holds him with his glittering eye,*
> *The wedding guest stood still,*
> *And listens like a three years' child,*
> *The Mariner hath his will.*

Go thou and do likewise.

Yours,

SIMEON STYLITES.

Delilah on the Hearth

Sir: I wish I could claim to have invented the title above as a description of some wives, but it comes from Holbrook Jackson. He uses it to describe Mrs. Samuel L. Clemens, who spent a good deal of her time giving Mark Twain a literary haircut, shearing the strength from his literary style.

It is, of course, not chivalrous to call any wife a Delilah. That is a fighting word. Yet there have been wives (it is much safer to put it in the past tense) who have played the part of the Lady with the Shears — a Delilah on the Hearth cutting away her husband's strength and his native endowment for indiscretion. The modern Delilah's work with the scissors differs greatly in motive from that of the original in Samson's affairs. That one was a siren, up to no good. The wifely

Delilah loves her husband dearly — so dearly, in fact, that she wants to keep him from taking any risks to health, wealth, or reputation. In other words, she keeps him from life.

I wish I could read the memoirs of Mrs. Christopher Columbus, if she wrote any. I would not be at all surprised if she frequently wound her loving fingers in his dark locks and said in soothing tones: "Chris, you are foolish to go on that wild voyage to the Indies. Goodness knows what winds may blow up. Your last winter's overcoat isn't heavy enough. You'll get pneumonia. Besides, that little rowboat, the Santa Maria, leaks." She would have kept him at home. Snip, snip, snip. But he got away.

We do know that John Wesley had a Delilah on the hearth. She tried to stop those long, silly horseback rides all over England. But John could say, "My head is bloody, but unshorn." After one of her diatribes, he was all the more eager for boot and saddle. I wonder whether John ever preached on "a thorn in the flesh to buffet me." He could have done a honey on that!

A real-life Delilah at the fireside was Mrs. Nathaniel Hawthorne. Her loving watchfulness to keep her husband polite and elegant clipped the curls of his strength as a writer. She changed his writing, substituting "look" for "squint," "pool" for "puddle," "perceived" for "smelt," "sat" for "sprawled." She softened passages describing poverty or sickness. In fact, whenever a word of specific power appeared she clipped it with shears she called "good taste."

Edward A. Steiner once said that often the wife of a preacher will slip a silken B.V.D. under the hair shirt her husband wears, so that the poor dear shall not suffer. Sometimes Delilah is a demon housekeeper; the washing machine and the vacuum cleaner become the sun and the moon. So the prophet is smothered in home economics. His locks are sheared.

Often the wife of a man of great possible usefulness is so concerned for his health that she keeps him from doing anything notable with it. Frances Power Cobbe described the process of the trimming of the hair of strength in these words:

> The higher good of the husband occupies most wives comparatively little; and often a man who starts with a great many lofty and disinterested aspirations deteriorates, year by year, in a deplorable manner under the influence of a well-meaning and personally affectionate wife. She urges her husband to think of himself and his own interests, rather than the people and objects for which he was ready to sacrifice himself. "Do not go on that charitable errand today. You have a cold coming on. Tomorrow will do, or later." "Do not invite that dull old friend." "Do not join that tiresome committee." "Do refrain from confessing your unorthodox opinions."

The girl with the shears at work!

Sometimes when her Samson is about to flex his muscles in real fighting, Delilah puts in a "What will peo-

ple say?" And the native hue of resolution is sicklied
o'er with the pale cast of propriety.

I don't know what to say about Delilah. She is a
lovely girl and it is nice to have her around. Just keep
the shears out of her reach — down in the coal cellar,
perhaps.

                              Yours,

                                   SIMEON STYLITES.

'Remain Explosively'

Sir: Did you happen to notice in the public prints not
long ago that there was a violent explosion in a church
in New York state — unfortunately not in the pulpit
but in the boiler room? It did a lot of damage, tossing
the pews into all sorts of unorthodox positions.

The item made sad reading, but it did provoke the
thought of what a wonderful thing it would be to
have explosions in the people occupying the pews instead of in the basement under them. So a few of us
crackpots are organizing a Society for the Promotion
of Bigger and Better Explosions. Would you care to
be Grand Detonator?

Laurence Housman, a few years ago, came near to
proposing such a society. Dick Sheppard, in the midst
of his great years as rector of St. Martin's-in-the-Fields,
London, had written to him in a dejected mood, saying
that he was on the point of leaving the church because

he was sure that there was no place in it for a rebel like himself. Housman, though utterly outside the church, violently disagreed. He wrote back and urged Sheppard to "remain explosively within the church."

That is an alluring vocation — to "remain explosively within the church." It sounds a lot more exciting than the Men's Club or the Altar Guild or the Ladies Aid Society.

Of course, explosions are nothing new in the church, but they so often happen in the wrong place and for the wrong reasons. And not all explosions are to the glory of God.

Years ago there used to be a comic strip featuring the Terrible Tempered Mr. Bang, who had an infinite capacity for spontaneous combustion. Mr. Bang is a member of a great many boards of deacons. Every time his toes are stepped on he explodes; and Mrs. Bang, by a process of chain reaction, explodes also. But those are the wrong kinds of explosion.

The New Testament explodes all over the place. Here are a few loving words which the Apostle Paul used to people who were blocking the path of the gospel: "You son of the devil, you enemy of all righteousness, you whitewashed wall." Definitely not the language recommended by Robert's *Rules of Order*. Perhaps that is what is the matter with us. Could it be that we are taking our cue from the wrong textbook? It would be a shock in many places to displace Robert's *Rules of Order* by the New Testament, but it might be exciting. More churches die from lack of excitement than from lack of money. Perhaps St. Paul would be a more rousing parliamentary leader than the parliamentary St. Robert F. W. H. Myers in his poem "St. Paul" catches beautifully this aspect of the Apostle:

> *Then with a rush the intolerable craving*
> *Shivers throughout me like a trumpet call.*

A shiver is a lot better than *rigor mortis*.

Think of explosion in pew and pulpit over muddled thinking, over mouselike trepidation before Caesar and Mammon, over festoons of ecclesiastical red tape that become winding sheets, over the limp acceptance of racial exclusiveness, over the unholy trinity of mint, anise, and cummin. You could make quite a list. There was never a better time to begin. Here is pencil and paper. What are we waiting for?

Yours,

SIMEON STYLITES.

Too Young or Too Old

Sir: If your memory is still agile enough to travel back to the middle of the Second World War, you will recall a mournful ditty with the refrain, "They're either too young or too old." It blared forth from juke boxes and radios, the strident complaint of a girl that, with millions of young men in the army and navy, no one was left at home to take her places except children and grandfathers, "either too young or too old."

Something like that seems to be the theme song of far too many churches looking for ministers. It is rather a shock, to anyone who can still be shocked by anything, to note how the period of "greatest availability" for ministers has been narrowed at both ends. I am not mad, most noble Festus, but speak forth the words of truth and soberness when I say that many churches — or at least the Politburo selecting the minister — start with the dogma that a man is too young at 35 and too old at 40.

If this goes on for a few years, it will develop that the only "right" age for a preacher to be called to a church is six months between 36 and 37 years. Perhaps this can be scientifically narrowed still further, to a period of 25 minutes during his 36th year. In this way churches will skillfully eliminate two of the most priceless assets in their work — the energy, initiative, and imagination of youth, and the experience, wisdom, and maturity of middle age and elder years.

The snap judgment, "He's too young for a church like ours," would have eliminated recruits such as Charles H. Spurgeon, Henry Ward Beecher, George Whitefield, Joseph Parker. For that matter, most of the twelve disciples would have come under the ban. If baseball operated under the totalitarianism of the calendar, a manager would have said to a gangling farm boy of 19 years, named Bob Feller, "You sit on

the bench for ten years. Then, when you have developed rheumatism, and if you are patient, I may put
you in as a relief pitcher in some game that is hope-
lessly lost." Under that school of thought all the teams
would be second-division teams.

That is exactly what has happened to a great many
churches; they are second-division outfits through lack
of daring and courageous leadership. Often this is not
the fault of the churches themselves, but is due to the
arbitrary ruling of the ecclesiastical high brass.

The loss is just as great at the other end. Henry
Hallam Tweedy once said that a good many churches,
on looking for a minister, seem to take their motto
from the parable of the Prodigal Son: "Give me a kid,
that I may make merry with my friends." When a
church erects an arbitrary deadline at 50 years or
earlier, it removes itself from the possibility of using
great powers, judgment, mature skill in counseling,
deep understanding of religious experience — all im-
measurable assets of pastoral ministry. Perhaps there
is wisdom in an old adage, not found, I am told, in the
Good Book, but in another realm of thought: "Play
both ends against the middle."

As long as I am weeping on your shoulder, let me
dampen it with about six tears more. I am one of
many who are distressed over another shortening of the
season in the work of the church. It is the steady shortening in city churches of the period of full-strength
activity. The summer "letdown" used to be confined
to July and August. Now it frequently lasts from June

1 to October 1. Soon the period of Protestant church activity may be just six months, from mid-October to Easter, with two short spurts at Advent and Lent. It threatens to become as highly seasonal as ice skating or skiing.

A question in the Gospel of John asks, "Are there not twelve hours in the day?" We might well ask, "Are there not twelve months in the year?"

Thanks for a good cry.

Yours,

SIMEON STYLITES.

The Wayward Postman

Sir: Once upon a time there was a postman who had served his Uncle Sam faithfully for forty-five years, delivering the right mail every day to all the houses on his devious route. Neither snow nor slush nor summer heat nor bunions ever stayed him from the steady pursuit of his rounds. Every morning he delivered to Mr. Montague, the vice-president of the First National Bank, his copy of the *Wall Street Journal,* and to Andrei Engels, the Marxist shoemaker over on River street, his eagerly awaited *Daily Worker.* The beloved saint, Mrs. Barbara Heck (aged seventy-five), never failed to get her copy of the *Christian Advocate,* nor did Professor Crooks ever miss his weekly *Scientific American.*

Came the last day of the postman's official travels. As he started on his rounds, some imp of perversity whispered in his ear the alluring suggestion that it would be a lot of fun for once to get the mail all mixed up. The imp went on to point out that he had delivered the right mail for over 15,000 trips and surely was entitled to one joyous spree. Also, more subtly, the imp held out the vision of making a great contribution to social understanding in the city by getting people off their mental beat through a novel kind of reading matter.

So the postman carefully delivered to Mr. Montague the copy of the *Daily Worker,* to widen his mental horizon, and left a copy of the *Nation's Business* with the fiery radical, Mr. Engels. With the same high aim and a lift of soul, he deposited on the doorstep of the Methodist pastor a copy of the *Brooklyn Tablet,* the aggressive Catholic paper, and left for the astonished Father McGinness, pastor of St. Bridget's Church, copies of both the *Churchman* and *The Christian Century.* The superintendent of public schools received the current issue of *Racing Form,* and on Dr. Keen, the eminent surgeon, was bestowed a copy of *Science and Health, with a Key to the Scriptures,* addressed elsewhere. And so on to the end, opening up new vistas at every mailbox.

Thus far the original story. But from there on, there are two divergent endings. One version goes on to relate that the next day tensions were healed, misunderstandings cleared away. But higher critics have

insisted that this ending is spurious, being an inter-
polation by a later redactor, and that the true version
is that there were next day 279 violent complaints to
the post office, 9 cases of apoplexy, 14 cases of high
blood pressure, and numerous minor calamities. You
can take your choice.

Just the same, the postman had himself a good time,
and went into retirement in a blaze of glory. He had a
sound idea — that getting off one's usual beat may be a
definite means of grace. It can be done without benefit
of an inspired postman. Doesn't it say in the Good
Book to be mindful of the things of others as well as of
our own?

A rowing coach, a few weeks ago, explaining the defeat of his protégés, said genially, "The boys rowed too
long in one place." It could be.

Yours,

SIMEON STYLITES.

Wait for the Verb!

Sir: I have been accused of being a member of the
Society for the Resurrection of Old Jokes. I admit it.
My only excuse is that the old ones, like old friends, are
best. When you hear a really good one you know that
Chaucer told it, or more likely Homer.

Here, for instance, is the ancient wheeze about the
German sentence, which has leaped right into the

center of a lot of things, religious and political. It is the one about the two Germans who went to a meeting where the speaker was long and tiresome. "Let's go," said one. "No," said the other, "let's wait for the verb."

That gives a fair idea of German sentence structure all right. Mark Twain put it picturesquely:

> Whenever the literary German dives into a sentence, that is the last you are going to see of him till he emerges on the other side of his Atlantic with his verb in his mouth.

And James Russell Lowell, struggling with the native tongue as a student in Germany, thus described it:

> Aber potztausend Donnerwetter! What a language it is, to be sure! with nominatives sending out as many roots as that witch grass which is the pest of all child gardens, and sentences in which one sets sail like an admiral with sealed orders, not knowing where the devil he is going until he is in midocean.

Quite literally, in many ways, the world is waiting for the verb. There used to be a popular song, "All the world is waiting for the sunrise." Today a better one would be, "All the world is waiting for the verb." For that is the exact truth. In the tension between the West and the Orient, the Orient is "waiting for the verb," the act, which will give some point and meaning to loud-swelling words about racial equality. Asia has had nouns and adjectives enough, and Asians are getting tired of waiting for the verb. That is what most of the shooting is about, in case you didn't know.

It is the same with the whole matter of church union or even real co-operation. Take a conference like the recent one at Lund, Sweden. I was not there, so I am not bothered by such things as facts. But from all the reports one gets the notion that Lund was a great success in nouns and adjectives but a failure so far as verbs go. There were no verbs of action audible to the naked ear.

Someone asked Averell Harriman, that veteran of many European conferences, "How is your French?" He answered instantly, "My French is excellent, all except the verbs." (Anyone whose youth was marred by a struggle with French irregular verbs will sympathize with him.) His remark is often paralleled by, "Our religion is excellent, all except the verbs." The adjectives in it are wonderful — "holy," "sacred," "divine," "noble," and all the rest of the thesaurus. There are glittering nouns to match. But no great verbs. Yet there are great verbs in the Christian religion — "come," "follow," "go," "do," "be," "work," "fight." Millions of people are waiting for the verb to go with the noun "brother," the deed to make it more than a word.

The verb is the sinew of speech. The Founder of Christianity liked verbs. He said, "You know these things, blessed are you if you *do* them."

Yours,

SIMEON STYLITES.

Good Friday — and a Toothache

Sir: A very short story that deserves a high place on any list of Lenten reading is one by the Russian novelist Leonid Andreyev — "The Day of the Crucifixion," in the volume *The Crushed Flower,* published by Alfred A. Knopf. It is one of the shortest stories Andreyev ever wrote, only a few hundred words, but it has a bite that lasts for years. It embodies a striking bit of imagination, which is conveyed in the first sentence:

> On that terrible day when the universal injustice was committed, and Jesus Christ was crucified between robbers on Golgotha — on that day from early morning, Ben-Tovit, a tradesman of Jerusalem, suffered from an unendurable toothache.

The crucifixion is then described as it appeared to a man occupied with an almost exclusive preoccupation, a toothache. Once in a while he becomes dimly aware of the procession to the cross, but soon goes back to his own private woe. His wife urges him to look at the men on the way to their execution, as a means of diversion. Here is Andreyev's description:

> One of the men, he of the long light hair, in a torn, bloodstained cloak, stumbled over a stone

which was thrown under his feet, and he fell. The shouting grew louder, and the crowd, like colored sea water, closed in about the man on the ground. Ben-Tovit suddenly shuddered for pain; he felt as though someone had pierced a red-hot needle through his tooth . . . He groaned and walked away.

Afterward he is led by a friend to see "the criminals on the crosses," but he does not stay: "He was eager to finish the story of his toothache."

There is no need to tack a moral to that bit of art. But the author certainly meant us to drop it into our imagination. It brings the humbling picture of missing the meaning of Calvary through any kind of preoccupation.

There is a continuing crucifixion going on, where all that Jesus cared for, taught, lived for, died for is scourged and crucified. Take hold of the wings of the morning and flop around the earth — Korea, South Africa, India, many places in our own country — till you come back where you started from. Good Friday is here again. How sharply do we see the crucifixion that still goes on? Does it break through the excluding wall of our own private toothache? W. H. Auden has given a vivid and searching picture of a private preoccupation while a tragedy is happening:

> *We haven't the time — it's been such a rush —*
> *Except to attend to our own little push:*
> *The teacher setting examinations,*

The journalist writing his falsifications,
The judge enforcing the obsolete law,
The banker making the loan for the war,
The expert designing the long-range gun
To exterminate everyone under the sun,
Would like to get out, but can only mutter,
"What can I do? It's my bread and butter!" *

Lord, is it I?

Yours,

SIMEON STYLITES.

'You Must Relax'

Sir: The woman who found great comfort in "that blessed word, Mesopotamia," has long since passed to her reward. The word is no longer blessed. But other words have sprung up from time to time to work their spell. As of this moment the "blessed" word to large numbers of people, both clergy and those entirely without bell, book, and candle, seems to be "relax." Psychology, of the sound and charlatan varieties alike, has made a large gift to the vocabulary of religion by revealing the virtues of relaxation. One result is that the new gospel of getting relaxed threatens to run away with the whole show.

* From *On This Island,* by W. H. Auden. Random House, New York. Used by permission.

Someone once observed that "when a new idea gets into an unfurnished mind, it has the time of its life." The idea of relaxation has certainly been having itself a time in a great many unfurnished minds.

For the truth that one needs to relax to keep the mind and spirit from being snapped by taut stretching has lately been so stressed that it bids fair to blot out all other aspects of the Christian gospel. In some pulpits the New Testament seems in danger of being abbreviated to one word, that blessed word "relax."

A score of book titles proclaims the word or the idea: *You Must Relax, How Never To Be Tired, The Art of Relaxation.* Sermons follow suit. A series on "Peace, Poise, and Power in Perpetual Possession" is followed by another on "You, Too, Can Be Serene." When this kind of thing is poured on too steadily the result is that all tension is taken out of life. And there can be no true Christianity without tension. Take the tension out of the mainspring of a watch and you have beautifully "relaxed" steel; you also have a useless piece of junk. A person can become so relaxed, so free from all disturbance about anything, that he likewise is a useless piece of junk.

We will soon have a rewritten gospel, thus: "If any man would come after me, let him keep down his blood pressure"; "Go ye into all the world and relax."

The bulletin board in front of a church recently announced the sermon topic for Sunday: "How to Live a Serene and Successful Life." Fine. So long as we do not forget that our Master lived a disturbed and unsuccessful life. He was deeply disturbed and moved with compassion at seeing the crowd harassed and bewildered, like sheep without a shepherd. He seems never to have mastered the art of relaxation as so soothingly proclaimed in six easy sermons. He carried tension to the end. And he died on a cross.

Yours intensely,

SIMEON STYLITES.

The Bull Pen

Sir: Now that the baseball season is with us again and the joyous sound of wood against horsehide is heard over the land, I recall one of the high moments of my career. For I have had my moments. I once talked for half an hour with the manager of a Major League Baseball Team. True, he couldn't get away from me, as he was wedged in on the seat next to the window in a crowded railroad car, and I was on the outside seat.

We talked of curves, knuckle balls, and Texas leaguers, and finally reached the subject of the bull pen. The bull pen, as everyone except possibly Great-Aunt Matilda knows, is a space, usually fenced in, in a corner of the outfield, to which reserve pitchers are sent to "warm up" in view of the possible collapse of the pitcher when he can't find the plate or is being hit all over the lot.

I asked the manager what effect it has on a pitcher

when he sees another pitcher warming up to take his place. He said that some pitchers get more jittery than ever and begin dealing out bases on balls with generous abandon, while others tighten up and sail the ball over the plate with the deadly aim of an Annie Oakley. It must be a tough place for a pitcher to be in, hearing the thump of the ball in the catcher's mitt out in the bull pen and realizing that any pitch may be his last for that game.

Then I got to thinking what might happen if the bull pen were introduced in other realms than baseball. What effect would it have on a preacher if he knew there was another man warming up out in the Sunday-school room, ready to step into the pulpit and displace him whenever his points got going wide of the congregation? The chances are, I think, that most preachers would not go to pieces, but would pitch with fresh fervor and drive, with speed, curves, and control. A bull pen in a church might be a means of grace.

Or how would an editor feel if he came across the office boy warming up out in the cloakroom, batting out on the old Hammond typewriter an editorial on America's foreign policy to take the place of the one the editor was writing mid toil and tribulation? What effect would it have on a businessman or a teacher if he knew that the next room was a bull pen in which his successor was getting ready to take his place?

Of course, that is just what is happening everywhere. Josephine Lawrence in her novel, *The Sound of Running Feet*, portrayed vividly the feelings of people in an office fearing that any day they might be motioned to the bench and someone else put into their job. The running feet were not those of a Hound of Heaven, but of a Hound of Elsewhere — the feet of someone running to take over their job.

Perhaps the bull pen is responsible for a large part of the good work being done in the world. It keeps us on our toes. We can readily see the disastrous effects that often come from a lifetime tenure of a job. Church history would be very different if there had been no life offices, if all popes and archbishops had been forcibly retired in the seventh inning.

By the way, who is warming up in your office to take the place of

Yours,

SIMEON STYLITES?

The Pulpit Committee

Sir: We have it on the authority of William Cowper that

> *God moves in a mysterious way*
> *His wonders to perform.*

If mystery is a hallmark of divinity, the pulpit committee of a church seeking a pastor must be a divine instrument, for it frequently moves in very mysterious ways — in ways that are dark and with tricks that are vain.

Often the members do not start with a job analysis to determine what capacities are needed in a leader for their situation. They set out on a vague search for an archangel, a combination of St. Francis of Assisi, Henry Ward Beecher, and Henry Ford.

The first step is to get a list of prospects. This will run to thirty or fifty names, including the wizard three thousand miles away so violently recommended by the second cousin of Mrs. Elmendorf's niece, three men recommended by bishops, two lame ducks brought upon the scene by various officials, and sixteen men who have nominated themselves.

Then on a Sunday morning five of the committee approach the church where the suspect is preaching. To insure secrecy, they break up three blocks away and enter the sanctuary one by one, with a nonchalant air, as though they had never seen each other. This procedure makes them as inconspicuous as a herd of elephants hiding behind a head of lettuce.

They look and listen, and sometimes sniff. Probably they do not pay too much attention to the sermon, for they are not really looking for a preacher. They are looking for some kind of organizational bulldozer, a high-powered promoter, whether he has much to promote or not; or for an ecclesiastical Luther Burbank, who can make four organizations grow where only one grew before. The thought that unless a man can and will preach he will ultimately have little to organize never swims into their ken.

Perhaps they do not like the sermon. For it happens that the preacher is not ballooning up in the empyrean, but is doing, in plain, vigorous words, a workmanlike job on some parish need, such as the budget or the educational task of the church. They shake their heads inwardly — "Not eloquent enough for our church."

They note every detail of the service, from the minister's necktie to the gowns on the choir. Perhaps the soprano is having an off day; at least she is off key at critical notes. Or the ushers are not wearing carnations and cutaways that Sunday, thus failing to give the impression of Roxy theater ushers on parade.

So with heavy hearts the pulpit committee steal back in Indian file to their auto three blocks away. Next Sunday to fresh fields and pastures new. All too often, the very qualities in a preacher for which they should thank God and take courage become liabilities. Strange that the sound basis for a choice — what the man has done and what he is known to be by those who know him best — counts so little. With some pulpit committees, Phillips Brooks would have no chance at all against Bob Hope.

> Dejectedly yours,
>
> SIMEON STYLITES.

Men of Distinction

Sir: I can't make it go. For some time now I have been trying, after closing the door to my room and pulling down the shades, to look like the "Men of Distinction" whose Napoleonic features and majestic forms are paraded in technicolor every week in the advertising sections of the slick magazines. I sit in my chair with my shoulders squared and a tall glass of milk in front of me, but I don't look very distinguished. My suit is never pressed right and the high-powered-executive look is missing.

Yet my ponderings while I posed have brought forth a thought which I pass on free to the distillers. They haven't done more than scratch the surface of this "Men of Distinction" idea. There are a lot more men that by rights should be included in the gallery. There is the man in Baltimore, for instance, who has achieved the distinction of having been sent to the county jail eighteen times in five years on account of conduct he probably wouldn't have indulged in had he been sober. Eighteen times in five years may not hang up a world's record, but it is a distinguished score nevertheless. Then there is the man in Michigan who has achieved the distinction of having been divorced four times in eight years because of confirmed drunkenness (his own). These two certainly rate a place in the Highball Hall of Fame.

Of less spectacular distinction, but still worthy of notice, are certain minor contestants I can name — the man who has lost five jobs in eleven months owing to the flowing bowl or a smaller vessel, and my neighbor who has had his driving license revoked twice in fourteen months for driving while "under the influence." I am sure the distillers and their public relations counsels will immediately perceive the vast possibilities in adding these notables to their gallery. Their pictures, in appropriate costumes, would round out the record and make it less one-sided.

Other possibilities crowd the imagination. How about pictures to illustrate the persuasive slogans of the breweries? "Gulp's Beer makes neighbors neighborly." I saw a couple of neighborly neighbors the other day, swatting each other under the stimulation of Gulp's. Or consider the possibilities of "Whimsey — the Unhurried Whisky." I saw a client recently who looked as though he would be not at all hurried for the next forty-eight hours.

Let's have, too, some additions to the list of "Who's Who-ers who have switched to Muddle's Reserve." There is a lot more switching to be recorded. There is the man who switched his address to Cook County Hospital, Alcoholic Ward.

Yours for keeping distinctions clear,

SIMEON STYLITES.

'He Simply Got Up and Left'

Sir: Not long ago my heart leaped up when I beheld a few words in Arnold Bennett's *Journals*. That was strange, for of all the "unleapable" books, poor Arnold Bennett's *Journals* — mostly a glorified cash ledger — are the most pedestrian. Yet here are the stirring words. Under date of March 9, 1928, he writes: "John Buchan, invited for tea at 4:30, arrived 4:27. He is a thoroughly organized man. And at 5:15, he simply got up and left."

Think of it, "he simply got up and left"! May his tribe increase! How did he do it? There are times when everyone feels that the ability of a caller simply to get up and leave is the highest achievement of man since the discovery of fire or the invention of the wheel. No wonder they made John Buchan a lord! I hope they threw in an Order of Merit. Simply getting up and leaving is a highly meritorious performance, but, alas, often an impossible one.

Sometimes the caller seems to be built into the room, like a mammoth table with elephant legs, too big to be squeezed through the door. Sometimes he, or she (don't forget *she*), seems to be a ship stuck on the ways of a dry dock and unable to be launched into the water. Or he is like a figure on Keats's Grecian Urn, frozen into immortal immobility.

Frequently this unshakable stability is not a case of total depravity, though often the frayed mind can find no other explanation of it. The built-in caller usually does not, with malice aforethought, plan to spend the rest of his life — or eternity, for that matter — in your living room. It is just that his wit is petrified by the prodigious feat of getting up and going. Sometimes it looks as though the conversation — or monologue — is coming to an end, and you watch eagerly for signs of a period with which to punctuate it. But that is only a mirage. He punctuates with a comma, gets his second or twenty-second wind, and goes on.

Here are a few suggestions for easing a caller out of the house. A warning, however: I have tried most of them, and they don't work.

1. Go to sleep. This is often not hard to do. But it is a frail reed to lean on. The caller may be polite and wait patiently for you to waken, and meanwhile he can consolidate his position and dig in for the winter.

2. Try telepathy. Say firmly in your mind one hundred times, "Go home!" Extra-Sensory Perception ought to help. But I have never been able to get the hang of it. I must write to Dr. Rhine. However, don't take too much stock in this mind-over-matter stuff. Mind has no power over matter as durable as the endless caller.

3. Train your wife to get convulsions, with loud screams. This may scare the visitor. But there is a catch in it. He was probably a Boy Scout and will do his

good deed by staying and throwing cold water on her. She won't like it.

4. Have a concealed bomb in the room which you can set off by a wire in your chair. This is hard on the rugs and curtains.

5. Resign yourself to the will of God.

6. Ask your guest to have some refreshments, and serve a beaker containing one part Coca-Cola and seven parts tabasco sauce. I haven't tried this yet. Come up and see me sometime!

Yours,

SIMEON STYLITES.

'Teenie-Weenie'

Sir: I can't think of anything to write you about this week, so how about another chapter of my autobiography (all rights reserved)? One summer night all the folks on the porch got tired of playing canasta (who wouldn't?) and somebody introduced the old subject, always good for ten or fifteen minutes, "What is the most beautiful word in the English language?" All the trusty old stand-bys were entered in the race — "azure," "horizon," even "opalescent." ("Mother" and "home" and "heaven" were ruled out of bounds at the beginning.) As usual, the word that an Italian traveling in this country said was the most beautiful word he heard here, "cellar door," was mentioned. (No wonder he felt that way, for its fine liquid and vowel sounds make "cellar door" seem like something out of Dante.) As in the croquet game in *Alice in Wonderland*, everybody won and got a prize.

Then I introduced the reverse question, "What is the ugliest word in the English language?" There was quite a spell of ugly conversation, with no winners and no prizes.

But a few evenings later I was in a home where the mother was trying to persuade her small son to go to bed. Being a bright youngster he didn't want to go. So she started teasing him. "Come, dear," she wheedled, "just make a little teenie-weenie prayer." "There," I shouted to myself, "I have it! That's it, the ugliest word in the language — 'teenie-weenie.' "

Of course it isn't a word, but just part of the jargon that some deluded parents use to prevent their children from learning English. It is an ugly word because it pictures an ugly thing, the sin of scant measure. Isn't one of the troubles of our vexed world the fact that there are so many "teenie-weenie" people set in very large places? (I'll have to leave that out; you can't spare space for 175,000 words in one issue.)

Too many "teenie-weenie" prayers that never get out of the four walls of a solitary confinement cell. Fifty years of "Now I lay me down to sleep"! "Teenie-weenie" faith that never plumbs to any depths but skims around on the surface of things like a water bug. "Teenie-weenie" expenditures of thought and energy and money — people measuring out their service with the worried look of a butcher agonizingly watching the scales lest he give one twenty-fifth of an ounce too much of chuck steak. Life becomes an affair of cubic centimeters.

Uncounted billions for guns and tanks, gushing geysers of gold for bombs, and "teenie-weenie" sums for world recovery, which is the only thing that might deal with the festering evils that communism thrives on. Every day in every way we resemble more closely the dinosaur, seventy tons of armor plate and two ounces of brain. (Something to think about — the dinosaur became extinct.) Millions — or is it billions? — down the RFC rat hole, and "teenie-weenie" amounts for education.

The only remedy I can think of at the moment is the little biscuits in *Alice in Wonderland* that made her grow several sizes larger on the spot. Won't you write to the National Biscuit Company about that?

Yours,

SIMEON STYLITES.

Goops

Sir: The gaiety of nations — which has been in very short supply lately — suffered a big subtraction in the death of Gelett Burgess of blessed memory. His fame did not rest entirely on his immortal lines beginning, "I never saw a purple cow." He served his day in many

works of wit and wisdom. But two books of his were
not for me, nor for many distracted parents back in the
innocent days of the 'twenties, occasions of merriment,
but near-tragedies. They were entitled *Goops and
How To Be Them, A Manual of Manners for Polite
Infants, and A Goop Directory for Juvenile Offenders
Famous for Their Misdemeanors.*

In case you were not afflicted with children back in
those days, I can explain that "Goops" were imaginary
creatures invented and drawn by Mr. Burgess. They
had large round heads like overgrown grapefruit,
spindly legs, and mean dispositions. They were shown
doing all manner of preposterous misdemeanors, short
of manslaughter. And each episode was followed with
the good advice, "Don't be a Goop."

Well, so far, not so good. The kids ate it up. A bright
child can always avoid a moral. I'll bet the Greek kids
did that on Aesop. The description of the crimes to be
avoided opened up to the children's minds bewilder-
ing delights which they had never thought of at all till
the moralistic Mr. Burgess came along. I remember
one little girl who, after studying Mr. Burgess, had the
afternoon of her life throwing an ink bottle at the wall.
And a pestiferous boy who re-enacted the drawing of a
Goop pulling the tablecloth off the table, with a soul-
stirring crash of dishes.

I happened to be thinking of Mr. Burgess and his
Goops the other day while I was looking over a book of
so-called popular psychology (which in many cases

means charlatan psychology). It was one of the many What's-the-Matter-with-Me books published by the dozen every week. And as I read I made a discovery. I said, "Holy cow! The Goops again!"

The book described all the ills of the mind, soul, and disposition so convincingly that the reader would feel coming upon him the symptoms of diseases he never even heard of till he started reading up on how to cure them. He makes the acquaintance of "ambivalence" and is sure he has it, for he has a pain right above the stomach. One chapter asked point blank the terrible question, "Do you have phobias?" I answered back, "I never did have, except for trying to balance my bank book, but since reading your book I have all the 79 phobias you list."

In this psychological age, these "cures" all too often suggest the disease. They are like the old advertisements of quack medicines "Does your back ever get tired after cleaning house? Well, you've got it!" "Are you short of breath after running up two flights of stairs? So? You have heart disease. Only Smith's Stabilizer can save you!"

There are quite a lot of Goops in church these days — good, solid Christian extroverts, all upset by week-by-week prescriptions for psychological and spiritual ills that in their innocence they had never thought of. But when the practitioner in the pulpit bangs away at Twenty-nine Things the Matter with You and How to Cure Them, the symptoms multiply rapidly. I know a man who never really knew what the word "frustrations" meant until he heard five sermons on how to cure them. Now he's completely frustrated.

Yours,

SIMEON STYLITES.

Paging Mr. Thoreau

Sir: I wish Henry Thoreau could have lived to have heard about the momentous words which formed the first conversation that went over the new microwave radio relay system put in operation across the continent. That conversation was right up his alley.

The $40 million relay system was completed not so long ago. It consists of 107 steel and concrete towers set 30 miles apart between New York and San Francisco. The first call was placed by H. T. Killingsworth, vice-president of the American Telephone and Telegraph Company in charge of long lines. He called Mark Sullivan, president of the Pacific Telephone and Telegraph Company. Across the $40 million worth of steel and concrete towers set every 30 miles apart between New York and San Francisco, Mr. Killingsworth said, "Hello, Mark, how are you?" Mr. Sullivan replied, "Hello. I'm fine, thank you. And you?" Thus ended the first lesson. A $40 million medium of communication and a profound message, "I'm fine. And you?"

I think Thoreau was the first to bewail the incongruity between marvelous inventions and the trivial uses to which they are so often put. His term for it was "improved means to unimproved ends." His classic remark, made when the air was filled with applause over the marvel of the new transatlantic cable, was, "Yes, and the first news that comes over it will be that the Princess Adelaide has the whooping cough."

Our age of electronics has vastly improved on the improved means of Thoreau's day. We send a plane up in the air to do incredibly skillful flying, only to print on the sky the name of a cigarette. We use the microwave relay system across the continent, as one minister has observed, to achieve the sublime end that, on television, millions see Red Skelton fall flat on his face. MGM spends $7 million filming *Quo Vadis*. Let an expert, Bosley Crowther of *The New York Times,* take the stand to tell of the result: "Here is a staggering combination of cinema brilliance and sheer banality, of visual excitement and verbal boredom, of historical pretentiousness and sex." Seven million dollars' worth of banality!

On the other side of the Altantic a contemporary of Thoreau, Thomas Love Peacock, wrote of the "improved ends" of locomotives, just coming into general use, "Now everybody is going for the sake of going, and rejoicing in the rapidity with which they accomplish nothing."

You remember from your high-school days Macaulay's "Essay on Milton" with its doleful thesis, "As science advances poetry inevitably declines." Are we caught in a parallel to that tragic paradox — that as the aids to fullness of living multiply, the life they were to aid inevitably dwindles?

All right, you say, can't we do anything but howl a dirge by the wailing wall? The wailing wall has never been much of a success as an instrument of salvation.

The only thing I can suggest is that we might get some direction from Thoreau himself. His words are very much alive and in date, a sharp reveille for a stiff battle for the life of the mind and spirit against domination by improved gadgets. Here are words he wrote in 1854, but nothing written in 1952, just about a hundred years later, will match them in timely importance:

> I went to the woods because I wished to live deliberately, to front only the essential facts of life, and to see if I could learn what it had to teach, and not, when I came to die, discover that I had not lived. Our life is frittered away by detail. Simplify, simplify.
>
> If the day and the night are such that you greet them with joy, and life emits a fragrance like flowers and sweet-scented herbs, is more elastic, more starry, more immortal, that is your success.

Two high arts of life — subtraction and addition. Thoreau knew how to subtract from the outside and add to the inside.

Yours,

SIMEON STYLITES.

The Fifth Freedom

Sir: Once upon a time there were the Four Freedoms. Perhaps you saw pictures of them. Now I am writing you about the Fifth Freedom. It is a nice thing to have around if you can manage it. It liberates a person from some very galling bondages.

To come to the point (a hard trick for me), it is the Freedom from the Necessity of Being a Big Shot. Arise, ye prisoners of reputation, and make a jail break!

For the grim necessity of being a Big Shot results in a crippling form of solitary confinement. It is a self-imposed bondage, but none the less confining on that account. The victim is put on a slim diet of prestige and reputation, which has a vitamin content far lower than that of bread and water. And at the door of the cell there is always the leering question, "How am I doing?"

If one has always to be a Big Shot, that eliminates the finest luxury of life, the sheer fun of being yourself. That, of course, is an expensive luxury, but it is worth a high price. It is a heavy bondage never to be able to say something because you believe it, never to be able to do a thing for the uncomplicated reason that you think it is the right thing to do, but always to have to do everything with reference to the Big Shot obsession.

There is the politician who might be a statesman. He has really got good ideas which he confides secretly to his wife and perhaps to his chauffeur in a closed car. But he must watch his words and step to be sure that he does not get off the road to the next step toward the goal of being a really Big Shot. A reporter nails him: "What do you think of an ambassador to the Vatican?" He makes a forthright reply: "I am for liberty and union, one and inseparable, now and forever." That covers the subject. Another newspaper pest asks, with pencil in hand, "Mr. Cicero, what would you do, if elected, about inflation?" The seer draws himself up and speaks for posterity (and the next election): "I believe in life, liberty, and the pursuit of happiness" (applause). So in all the primaries there will be a resounding chorus of

> *Come weal, come woe,*
> *My status is quo.*

There must be a host of physicians whose understanding of the medical need in the United States, and concern for meeting it, runs far, far beyond that of the officials of the American Medical Association and its Washington lobby. Could it be that their need to be medical Big Shots with the right connections strikes them dumb with acute laryngitis, so that they cannot speak?

Then there is, here and there, the preacher who is never really free to go where his mind and heart desire because he is always busy baby-sitting with his reputation. He drags his ball and chain, figuring his chances for getting this or that promotion, so that he can hardly pronounce a benediction without reference to the odds on tomorrow's race.

There was once a preacher totally free from this bondage, and, by the best accounts, he had a wonderful time. He got a call to a church in Macedonia, at Philippi. There was no church there, but he had a call. He did not have to sit down, as some later apostles do, like a chess player and figure the effect of this move on two or three possible moves ahead. He did not have to ponder things like: "Of course, where I really want to get to is the First Church in Rome. Perhaps it would be better to hold off on Philippi and see if I cannot get a call to Grace Church, Corinth, for it will be a lot easier to get to Rome from Corinth than from a little one-horse church like Philippi." Things were simpler then. "When he had seen the vision, immediately we endeavored to go."

I have heard it rumored that a man once said, "He that findth his life shall lose it." Do you suppose that could be true?

Yours,

SIMEON STYLITES.

Homage to Button Gwinnett

Sir: Would you like to make $25,000? Here's a chance. Go up into your attic and drag out the old trunk under the eaves, get out the pack of yellowed letters, and see if your great-great-great-great-grandfather — or his lovely wife, for that matter — ever got any letters from a certain Button Gwinnett, signed legibly with his own name. If so, you can sell the autograph and retire from labor and devote yourself to paying your income tax.

Button Gwinnett has had a strange fate. His is not the most honored name in American history but, as you know, when it comes to the cash value of autographs, lo! Button's name leads all the rest. John Hancock's emphatic signature and Thomas Jefferson's neat device are a dime a dozen compared to Mr. Gwinnett's. His autograph is literally worth its weight in radium.

It is an irony that he died insolvent. He died far too soon, killed in a duel. He should have waited for a rising market. His story belongs in the short and simple annals of the poor. He was a London merchant who settled in Savannah, Georgia, in 1765, and was elected a delegate to the Continental Congress. He stayed in Philadelphia only a bit over three months, but he was one of the signers of the Declaration of Independence.

The reason for the fabulous value of his autograph

is, of course, scarcity. Collecting the autographs of the signers of the Declaration has become quite a sport, and no collection is perfect without Button's autograph. There are only 36 known autographs of his in existence. In 1925 his autograph was worth $14,000, and today its value is double that. The moral is clear: Write less and your words will be worth more.

I am trying to get a picture of Button Gwinnett to put on my desk. It might do a lot of good. It would say to me — and to anyone else — Go in for scarcity; write a lot less, and the market may rise like a beautiful bird!

I know what you are thinking — that if Simeon wrote one letter a year, someone might read it. I admit you have something there. If we all talked less, someone might listen. Why not try a little game of "Button, Button, who's got the Button"? Scarcity may be the very button on fortune's cap!

In that book of rich humor — alas, now forgotten — Lloyd Douglas's *The Minister's Everyday Life,* he commends the virtue of scarcity to the pastor going to a new city. He urges him not to spread himself all over the local zoo, speaking to the Lions, the Eagles, the Elks, and the Moose. If anyone wants to see and hear the new curiosity, let him come to the one place where the man is on exhibition, his church.

The $25,000 price on Mr. Gwinnett's autograph whispers compellingly to every public speaker: The fewer words, the higher value. There are two styles of public speaking, the antediluvian, when everyone lived to a ripe old age of 700 or so, and the postdiluvian, when folks have only threescore years and ten, so they have to get to the point.

I can hear you muttering, "If this letter were a lot shorter, it might be a bit better." True! So here's to Button Gwinnett!

Yours,

SIMEON STYLITES.

The *Ding an Sich*

Sir: Once upon a time I started out to get an education. Don't interrupt to ask me why I quit. That is what I am going to tell you. Working one summer as a somewhat Able Laborer, third class, I thought every ten minutes that there must be easier ways to make a living. So I set out to learn something.

I started in on philosophy, and got as far as Kant. I couldn't understand that, so I quit philosophy. Then I switched to economics and got as far as Money. I couldn't understand that, either theoretically or practically, so I quit economics. Then I quit, period. There were no faculty objections.

But I remember three words from the course on Kant — *"Ding an sich."* (Not a bad score for a half-year, three times a week.) More than that, I can translate the words: the "thing in itself." I do not know what they meant to Kant; I never learned what anything meant to Kant. But, honest, they have meant plenty to me, and to a lot of folks.

The really lucky people are those who can do a thing for the interest and joy in the "thing in itself," without much, or any, concern for the trimmings that go with it. With some folks, this flair for the thing in itself is a gift; with some, it is an achievement. But however it comes, it is the Grand Prize.

This is true, for instance, of physicians. There are a few whose chief concern is prestige, shining equipment, crowded waiting rooms, and crowded safe deposit boxes. With the great majority, praise be, it is something quite different: the practice of medicine. They have chosen the better part, on the sheer basis of fun and excitement, in spite of contradictory monthly statements from the First National Bank.

There are some teachers who go in primarily for the upholstery of education — the rung on the academic ladder, arranged like the Hindu caste system; the rate of pay increases and vacation time. There are others, poor simple souls, who get their fun out of teaching — the thing in itself, the mystery of communication which can never be recorded on the payroll or in *Who's Who in America*. A classic picture of these is Louis Agassiz standing at a blackboard, a piece of chalk and a clamshell in his hand, no more concerned with his world-wide reputation than with whether his shoes are shined or not, having the time of his life before a small audience of farmers.

Art has the same two classes. When Turner painted

his pictures of sunsets, he was not looking at the chance of selling the canvas for a possible thousand pounds. Ten to one, he was looking at a sunset.

The fateful wide chasm divides preachers also. A great artist in words once described religious leaders who were much more feverish over the paraphernalia than over the thing in itself. He pointed out three dangers besetting prophets. He said: "They love the places of honor at feasts, and the best seats in the synagogue, and being called Rabbi." There you have it, today as in the far yesterday — all hot and bothered about the trimmings. Places of honor — elected to something or other on the first ballot, or any ballot; being chairman of something, even if it is only of the Committee on Complimentary Resolutions. The best seats — any seat with inner-spring cushions.

All such win some of the most terrible words ever pronounced: "They have their reward." They got what they wanted. Paid in full. No mysterious remainders still to come. They miss the real thing.

You pays your money and you takes your choice.

Yours,

SIMEON STYLITES.

No Boswell, Please!

Sir: The volume of James Boswell's *London Journal* (unquestionably the pornographic success of 1950) starts various reflections about James Boswell, Esq. I do not want to get into that, because you know how hard it is for me to keep to the point, even where there is one. What I am writing to tell you is that, on the basis of several recent books of recollections about this person and the other, I have unanimously concluded that a Boswell, gathering up for public view all one's occasional inanities and idiocies, either before or after one's death, is an unmixed calamity. One of the great joys of total obscurity is that there will be no danger of the recordings of a Boswell. Boswell may have been all right for Sam'l Johnson. But a Boswell can ruin almost anyone else if he is diligent enough. Emily Dickinson had the right idea:

How dreary to be Somebody!
How public like a frog!

So I say roughly, "No Boswell, please!"

What has brought on this outburst is the recent book *Thirty Years with Bernard Shaw,* by Blanche Patch. Miss Patch out-Boswells Boswell in tenderly preserving for posterity some of the silliest remarks ever made. She certainly done her hero dirt. Here are a few of the brightest gems, rescued from oblivion where they surely belong. "The belief in God's love," said the Great Sage, "is a lot of charming flapdoodle." How terrible to have had that aphorism lost through having no Miss Boswell present to catch it in a basket! Shaw attends the installation of the rector of the church at Ayot St. Lawrence and calls it "a great farce." Here's another: "He [Shaw] set aside St. John's vision of the second coming and the Great Judgment as 'ravings.' " Methodism, he declared, "is the most abhorrent and debasing form of religion that exists." It is good to have that cleared up! Again, he announced, "I have no patience with dogma in any form." (The only tolerable dogma was that of the Infallibility of Bernard Shaw.) A final example: "The idea of personal immortality scared him. 'The horror of it would drive you mad,' he said." (So it would if immortality were just an egotistical prance through the millenniums.)

Exhibit closed. How would you like to have a little Boswell at your side with pad and pencil?

Other books raise other terrors. They demonstrate that a person can be his own Boswell if he leaves his casual letters around. Here, for instance, are some gems of serene ray from this year's book, *The Letters of Theodore Roosevelt:* "Henry James was a miserable little snob." "The works of Chaucer were often just obscene." "William Jennings Bryan resembles Thomas Jefferson, whose accession to the presidency was a terrible blow to the nation." Exit Jefferson.

That scares me. I'm going to quit writing letters to you (applause) or to anyone else, to avoid being my own Boswell. All my executors will ever find is such letters as this:

UNITED BUTCHERS, LTD.:

I enclose check, but must say that $2 a pound for decayed shoe leather is outrageous. Disrespectfully yours —

BOOK-OF-THE-HOUR GUILD:

I am returning your selection *From Here to Eternity*. I learned all the swear words of World War I and cannot see that those of World War II open up any new lines of thought.

Yours on the safe side,

SIMEON STYLITES.

'Late Bloomers'

Sir: I have not been officially authorized by the Amalgamated Youth of America to award a Distinguished Service Medal with Crossed Palms to President Charles W. Cole of Amherst College. But I was never one to stand on formalities; I will volunteer. For in his address at an anniversary meeting of the College Entrance Examination Board, Dr. Cole rendered distinguished service to a lot of frustrated youngsters. As a result, history will doubtless take a new turn.

All the downtrodden kids whose lives have been blighted by flunking college board examinations will yell themselves hoarse over the belated appearance of a champion for their case against fate. They always knew there was something wrong with the college boards, and here comes an LL.D. saying, "Boys and girls, you were right. There *is* something rotten in the state of Denmark, New York, Illinois, Texas, and Hollywood." He said that the students who receive mediocre or poor grades, very often later become distinguished leaders. He said that the college admission system has put a premium on precocity, favoring those who mature early. He also suggested (oh happy thought!) that many of the geniuses who come through with an average of 96.7 per cent have frequently shot their whole intellectual wad and will never fire again. The colleges, he said, should pay more attention to the "late bloomers" who get a slow start in the spring but before snow falls proliferate into roses the size of sunflowers. (Free translation.)

Sweet music! Play it again! If I had only heard about the "late bloomers" in my misspent high-school days! Then, when I had to face the report that I got 62 in English, 57 in French, and 45 in algebra, I would have had a snappy comeback. I would have said, squaring my shoulders and looking her straight in the face, "Miss Minerva, you are all wet. Your educational theory is behind the times. I am not a moron, as you ignorantly insist. I am one of the late bloomers, and President Cole says we are the white hope of civilization."

What a shot in the arm this news will be to a great host of mothers and fathers! With what agonizing concern they have followed the little craft of Tommie and Jane as it was tossed about in the educational whirlpool, far more turbulent than the Niagara river below the falls. They might pose for a picture of Hope, like the one by Watts, with only one string left on the harp; troubled by every report card, yet not distressed; perplexed, but not in despair; cast down, but not destroyed. Now they can lift up their hearts with the discovery that nature goes in for late bloomers. Teacher's verdict of "lunkhead" on Tommie is premature. The returns are not all in yet. So they can twang that one string again and make music out of it.

In fact, there is a higher authority for late bloomers than even President Cole. It says: "Be not weary . . . for in due season ye shall reap, if ye faint not." Also, in my new translation of the New Testament (everyone is taking a whack at it; why shouldn't I?) it says, "If the vision of Tommie and Jane as top-flight performers tarry, wait for it."

Yours,

SIMEON STYLITES.

'Ministers of Grace'

Sir: If you ever get really mad — say when you are trying to put the paper to bed and it won't go — and need some good, round, mouth-filling and soul-satisfying oaths, let me recommend the reading of William Shakespeare. He was a man of infinite resource in that line. He didn't depend on the parrotlike repetition of common profanity, which, in his day as in ours, springs from a lack of vocabulary and a lack of brains. If, as Byron asserted, the "loud laugh proclaims the vacant mind," the loud oath proclaims a complete mental vacuum. No, sir, William was an artist. He could make his own. And very pretty ones many of them were, too. You could use them at a Sunday-school picnic and when you went to call on your grandmother — a handy kind to have.

One in particular that I like is in *Hamlet* — "Angels and ministers of grace defend us!" If you get your chest tones into that you can scare folks with it. Any good oath has to be theological, and this one is crammed with orthodox theology.

It is worth taking a second look at. We all need "ministers of grace" to defend us from the risks of life. There are many strange ministers of grace that do not look at all like angels, but do defend us from falling into a pit.

Failure is a real minister of grace which may defend us from the calamity of becoming insufferable asses. How intolerable we would all be if we had never made a sorry mess of things and thus kept active our membership in the human race and our understanding of people! If we had never made a whopping failure, God himself could not stand us, to say nothing of the neighbors. If a person has never been anything but a Big Booming Success, he can never do anything but "boom" the rest of his life. But if he has known the humiliation of failure, he may become fit to live with.

Pain is a minister of grace to people. No one ever ought to write about pain unless he has a toothache, an earache, and sciatica at the time he is writing. Then he would be worth listening to. But even the shortsighted can see that pain has been to many people a real minister of the grace of sympathy. Gelett Burgess, in his priceless little book *The Educated Heart,* describes this ministry. He says that you greet a friend with a casual "How are you?" and he answers, "I've had a bad case of lumbago." You hastily mutter, "Too bad," and hurry on. It has made no more impression than rain on a slate roof. Then *you* get lumbago, and plenty of it. Your voice when you meet your friend has a new inflection. "How about that case of lumbago you had last year? I hope it's better. What did you do for it?"

A sense of humor is a minister of grace. It is closely related to religious faith in that both give one a sense of proportion, a perspective on oneself. It acts as Charles Lamb says April Fool's Day acts, and says, "You look wise. Pray correct that error." Canon B. H. Streeter makes clear this service of humor when, in the midst of a heavy theological argument, he tells the story of two London cabbies watching a lordly figure descend the steps of a mansion. "He glittered when he walked." One cabman says to the other, "Bill, did you ever hear of God?" The other admits that he has. "Well," says the first, "that's Archibald, his brother." Without a sense of humor which forces us to laugh at ourselves, we are all on our way to the horrid fate of becoming "Archibald," God's brother.

Yours,

SIMEON STYLITES.

Knowing the Right People

Sir: Did you ever read a novel and forget everything about it except a little picture, and that not the chief thing the book was about? Yes, I know you are surprised that I remember anything at all, but I really do remember this. I forget even the name of the book; it was Something about a Village by Francis Brett Young.

There were three daughters who lived in a swanky community in England, called "The Grange." They were the local big shots, because they had been "presented" at court. They were so anxious to know nobody but the right people that they knew practically nobody at all. I guess that makes the punishment fit the crime, all right! Funny thing about it, that is not fiction, but fact. That is the way it works out.

Besides, they got the short end of the deal, for knowing only the right people is dull business. The right people are frequently the wrong people — from any standpoint of human enjoyment. You can exchange calling cards with them, but, Lord help us, what else? Old Professor Wilson of Edinburgh, who wrote under the name of Christopher North, said frequently he thanked the Lord that he never lost his taste for bad company.

A little girl in England not long ago proved to be a

sharp observer. After being told endlessly that if she were good she would go to heaven, she asked her mother pleadingly, "If I am really good in heaven, may I have some little devils to tea?" Sounds like a big party and a lot more exciting than prim angels playing on harps.

Didn't you ever know a church that died from just knowing the right people? That is why most churches that die do die. They are like those withering daughters at The Grange in the story, playing endless games of cribbage and bridge in their decorated drawing room or driving through the village in an isolation as solitary as Napoleon's when he took the air at St. Helena. These churches were so afraid of knowing the wrong people that gradually they knew nobody and became mausoleums. Every city has a few of them. In many cases the right people, socially and financially, moved away, and they could not, of course, take in the wrong people, so they took in nobody. These wrong people had nothing to recommend them except that they were God's children and that Christ died for them.

The whole tragic problem of social distance has a base in the fear of knowing the wrong people. Sticking with one group of like-minded people behind self-erected stockades is a cause of social isolation and of the tragedies it leads to. We are having much discussion these days on getting in touch with the moon. But what many persons and groups need most is to get in touch with the earth. That means having a number of the wrong people on your calling list. Otherwise any group, be it in the overstuffed lounges of the Union League Club or the cushioned pews of First Church or the stiff-backed chairs of the C.I.O. or A.F. of L. local, becomes a group of shut-ins.

Was not one of the chief indictments of Jesus that he did not know the right people and circulated among the riffraff of publicans and sinners? In the parable of the last judgment was not the condemnation given to those who were told, "I was hungry and ye gave me no food . . . sick and in prison and ye did not visit me" — essentially, that they did not know the right people?

Yours,

SIMEON STYLITES.

'Hi, Brother!'

Sir: Ordinarily I prefer the sports columns to the obituary columns. But being a working member of the human race, I occasionally let my eye stray to the obituary page. Several times I have come across entries like this: "She was a member of the Daughters of the American Revolution, of the Society of Mayflower Descendants, and of the Order of Colonial Dames." Whether she ever did anything else is not revealed.

There seems to be quite a clan of people whose chief

business in life one might describe as being "professional descendants."

All that follows here you can put down as sour grapes. For my ancestors did not come over on the Mayflower. They missed the boat by 150 years. But I am broad-minded. Being a descendant is a good profession. It is fairly easy, with no laborious training required. You meet such interesting people, and it gives you a heady feeling of superiority to the mill run of the human race.

But to be a professional descendant in good standing demands two techniques, both, alas, faulty.

For one thing, you must pick out *one* ancestor and disregard all the others. For instance, Mrs. Norman is a descendant of William the Conqueror. She must blink entirely the fact that she may also be a descendant of Bill the Conquered, a promising young highwayman of Hounslow Heath who likewise attained a high position in England — to wit, ten feet off the ground at the end of a rope. John Godfrey Saxe, many years ago, whispered a confidential word to our "best" families:

> *Depend upon it, my snobbish friend,*
> *Your family thread you can't ascend*
> *Without good reason to apprehend*
> *You may find it waxed at the farther end*
> *By some plebeian vocation.*
> *Or worse than that, your boasted line*

May end in a loop of stronger twine
That plagued some worthy relation.

The second necessary technique which gives you the right to raise your eyebrows and look down your nose at your neighbors is to assume that all your ancestors were exclusively your own. Once you let go your hold on that fallacy, the whole family tree comes down with a crash, as though an Oklahoma twister had playfully brushed it in passing.

Burgess Johnson in his autobiography, *As Much as I Dare,* has let loose a mathematical hurricane on all family trees. All right, he says, let's assume that you, Mr. or Mrs. Descendant, have an exclusive ancestry, and that your family line never crossed that of any of the lower orders. "If any genealogical graph were as simple as the branching of a tree," he writes, "an American of pure English ancestry would have had, at the time of the Magna Carta, 265 trillion, 890 billion, 889 million, 094 thousand, 649 ancestors."

Quite a lot of forefathers! If you don't believe it, go up to the attic and get out your old arithmetic book, turn to the section on arithmetical and geometrical progression, and start playing with it.

But that is only a drop in the bucket, and it is a big bucket. Suppose that 40 million people in the United States had at least one English ancestor (and that may be well within the mark) and that they were all exclusive — that would give you something like 20 million times 265 trillion. Well, you do it yourself; I'm getting dizzy. The fact is that in A.D. 1215 there were not more than eight million people in England to serve as ancestors. "The true genealogical tree reveals branches growing together at the tips as well as the trunk." That means we all have substantially the same ancestors. How does it happen that "professional descendants" never stumble onto this fact?

In other words, my dear sir, you *are* my brother, whether you like it or not. It's a tough break, but you might as well face the mathematics. Perhaps this throws some light on the resounding phrase, "the brotherhood of man." It is not the pious, sentimental nonsense that some people account it, but the basic biological fact, no more nonsensical than the multiplication table.

I have the honor, sir, to remain,

Your brother,

SIMEON STYLITES.

'Whatever Is Worth Doing . . . '

Sir: I have decided to devote the rest of my life to combating the deleterious effects of ancient proverbs, masquerading as wisdom, which exert a totalitarian tyranny over what ought to be free minds. There are many old wives' fables which have achieved a moral authority greater than that of the Ten Commandments.

I am pointing my opening gun at an old adage which has been a deep distress to my congenital awkwardness: "Whatever is worth doing at all, is worth doing well." That is nonsense of purest ray serene. There are a hundred things that are worth doing provided you don't bother about doing them well. That spoils the sport! If you go into a nervous breakdown about doing things right up there near to perfection, you lose your amateur standing — a priceless boon — and become a tiresome professional.

I know a man who gave up golf because some ancient fool had said, "Whatever is worth doing at all, is worth doing well." He should have stood on his rights and pointed out the undebatable truth that the man who doesn't play golf well gets twice as much fun and exercise as the man who plays it very well; he hits the ball twice as many times. It stands to reason that if Gene Sarazen turns in a card of 72 strokes, I get twice as much fun for the same money by swatting the ball 144 times. Q.E.D.

Is there any torture worse, for a regular member of the human race, than to play contract bridge, or even canasta, with three eager beavers who insist on doing it well? Can't a person relax playing bridge without becoming that fiend in human form, Ely Culbertson?

The false authority of this old wheeze about doing it well or not doing it at all is partly responsible for the disappearance of the active voice from a large part of American life. This is a grave matter. Too many people have traded their birthright as active performers for a mess of pottage — looking at professionals who "do it well." We are sinking down into the passive voice. We have traded all the bounce and gladness of *doing* something for the sodden inertia of looking at something or listening to something.

We see this as clearly in music as anywhere else. No wonder a wise child once shrieked out at a concert, "Look, mamma! A man playing the piano with his own hands!" The child knew that that was terrific. Douglas Gilbert, in his diverting book *Lost Chords*, puts it sharply: "America is no longer a melodic nation. We do not sing any more. We are sung at."

I forget who it was that said some years ago that what America needed badly was "more poor music." A toast to him! He meant that we need more music in the home created on the spot for the sheer fun of it. When we were not so vicarious in our music there were pianos in homes, and Bill, Fred, and Mabel made music, not Decca, Victor, and Columbia. Can you remember (Don't say Yes — it will date you) a ballad called "Maggie Murphy's Home":

> There's an organ in the parlor
> That gives the house a tone,
> And you're welcome every evening
> At Maggie Murphy's home.

Here's to Maggie Murphy! It was homemade music that helped to make a house a *home,* and not merely a point of departure for the movies or the jukebox.

J. B. Priestley hits the bull's-eye in his "Rain on Gad's Hill":

> Chesterton once shrewdly observed that there was a great difference between an eager man who wanted to read a book, and a tired man who wanted a book to read. It is the difference between active and passive amusement. Now we have too many tired persons who merely want a book to read, a film to stare at, a wireless program to listen to, and to be smothered in stuffy comfort while they are doing it.

And don't forget that this "doing it well" nonsense has kept more people from doing a needed job in the Kingdom of God than all the assaults of the devil.

Yours,

SIMEON STYLITES.

Footnotes

Sir: No, you are wrong. This letter is not a diatribe against footnotes which break out like a rash of measles all over the page. I get used to them. Besides, the world is getting better in that respect. There are far fewer footnotes today in books that are meant to be read. They are more confined to Ph.D. theses and monographs and such bleak geological formations.

I am appearing as a cheer leader for footnotes. Here is the idea. A reviewer of a volume of letters by Robert Browning wrote, "A curious fact is that many of the editor's footnotes make better reading than the letters they explain." Brother, that is not curious at all! That is life, and it is one of the nicest things about life. The footnotes are very often much more interesting and valuable than the main text. Of course, that happens sometimes in books. In that respect Van Wyck Brooks is my favorite author. He has a lovely way with footnotes. It is as though he shakes the tree and all the ripest plums, all the jokes and the wisecracks, drop from the top of the pages into the footnotes below. A very lively book could be made out of the footnotes in the Brooks series, beginning with *The Flowering of New England.*

The exciting thing about life in general is this, that very, very often the incidental thing, the unsung event, the thing passed over, turns out to be more important than the text. Take Sydney Smith, for instance. The official text of his life is that he was a clergyman who never obtained the posts for which his abilities fitted him. He was a disappointed man. His principal occupation seems to have been eating dinners. But what footnotes! A whole aurora borealis of wit and humor! Forked lightning sometimes; a warm summer afternoon of humor at others. Infinitely better than the rather dull prose of his official life.

We knew a woman whose official life story could be

put in one sentence, thus: "She was a farmer's daughter who, after graduating from high school, became the wife of a grocer and died at the age of 72." That is all — short enough to go on a small gravestone. But O Boy, or better O Girl, what footnotes! The salt and pepper that was in her, and that she sprinkled joyously around her all her life! The pepper that kept at bay for a week a baffled crew of surveyors for a new road through her property! And the salt. Doesn't the Bible say, "Let your conversation be flavored with salt"? If not, it ought to; one of the biblical authors just forgot to put it in. And the well-concealed kindnesses tucked in as little footnotes!

This is not just a foolish whim of mine. It's in the Bible. The big meaning of the parable of the Last Judgment in the 25th chapter of Matthew is that life is truly measured by its footnotes. Listen to the astonishment — "When saw we thee hungry and did not feed thee?" Or even more surprised, "When did we see thee hungry and fed thee?" It had all been in the unconscious footnotes, not in the public text in big print.

More than that, the Muse of History — good old Clio — has a mischievous sense of humor. She arranges it that the footnotes of yesterday become the headlines of tomorrow. Just take a sample. In August 1859 Charles Darwin's *Origin of Species* was published with a noise like that of a rose leaf dropping to the ground, while all London was agog over the visit of Tom Thumb to Queen Victoria. Clio must have laughed

hard at that one. So cheer up. The footnotes of today
may well be the headlines of tomorrow.

                              Yours,
                                   SIMEON STYLITES.

Take a Letter to Yourself

Sir: I notice that the latest item for the devotees of
Kafka, *The Diaries of Franz Kafka,* 1914–23, is described by several reviewers as "a series of letters to
himself." I can only hope that when he received them
he could understand them better than I can. I can
follow him only a very short distance.

That reminds me that we do write letters to ourselves, quite a well-kept-up correspondence, even
though we do not mail them and so save a lot of
postage.

The trouble is that most of our interself letters carry
too much comfort, when often a well-placed kick
would be more in order and contribute more to our
salvation. Too many of our letters to ourselves run
like this:

You Poor Dear: It was a dirty shame you were
not elected president of the Village Improvement
Association last night. You deserved it a thousand
times more than the complete moron who was
elected. It was all due to spite and jealousy. But

remember that the greatest minds were never recognized, and your defeat proves that you are a great mind. Think of Keats and Galileo.

Your unfailing admirer,
Yourself.

That can grow into a twenty-year correspondence. Here's another we frequently send:

Dear Atlas: You can't carry the world on your thin shoulders any longer. It is too heavy. You are working yourself to death. You have lost weight and are down to a mere shadow at 255 pounds. Do take care of yourself.

Your constant well-wisher,
Me.

Why not try a different sort of letter, just for variety? It might counteract the glut of too much soothing sirup. How about something like this:

You Big Bluff: I have been looking over your income tax report for last year. Don't leave town; you won't go to jail, but the figures ought to make you hide your head in a rain barrel. I see that you took the government's blanket deduction for interest, taxes, and contributions combined as being more financially advantageous than to list your contributions separately. That means that your contributions to all causes were so small as to be not worth recording. You did not live up to even the government's idea of what a decent man might give away. Don't speak to me for a year.

Not very cordially
Your Anemic Conscience.

And this might help:

Dear Demosthenes: Your speeches are getting worse and worse. I have been following you around and note that you have told the story of George Washington and the cherry tree in your last seven efforts. If you had been listening to anything else except yourself you could have heard the groans of the Rotary club four blocks away. Everyone else did. Either get some new stuff, or shut up. Try the second alternative first.

You Know Who.

Anyhow, I am going to write some letters to

Yours,
SIMEON STYLITES.

Too Many Shrines

Sir: Have you noticed it too? You can hardly pick up a newspaper these days and not find in it a story of the dedication of some new shrine. We seem to be going in for holy places in a big way. Here a shrine, there a shrine, everywhere a shrine. I am expecting any day now to read in the *Daily Blast* this dispatch:

PANTHEON, IND. — (AP) The National Tiddlywinks Shrine, costing $200,000, was dedicated
here yesterday, in the presence of 10,000 members
of the American Tiddlywinks Association. It was
erected in honor of Obadiah Snap, the founder of
the game of tiddlywinks. It is built of Indiana
limestone, and it surrounds a High Altar on
which is displayed the first set of tiddlywinks invented by Mr. Snap.

We have had for some years the National Baseball
Shrine with its Hall of Fame at Cooperstown, New
York, dedicated to the hallowed memory of Mr. Abner
Doubleday, who may or may not have invented baseball. It has a Pantheon far surpassing the one at Paris,
for what, after all, are Voltaire and Hugo compared
to Christy Mathewson and Babe Ruth? Now there is,
or is to be, a Professional Football Shrine. Even college fraternities are no longer content, as in the old
days, to try to collect dues to pay the mortgage, but
have become religious institutions, with shrines in
which to genuflect to the Noble Founders. (If you
don't believe it, run out to Evanston some day.)

These shrines are more than the familiar historical
markers, such as dot every crossroads in Virginia: "On
this spot, General Epaulet stopped for a drink before
the battle of Chancellorsville"; or, "George Washington woke up here and couldn't find his spectacles."
This shrine complex is something different.

I'm worried. I wonder if this wholesale hallowing is

the inevitable accompaniment of an increasing secularization of American life. The human mind, like the
rest of nature, abhors a vacuum. So when the High
Altar of God is either completely or partially dis-
mantled in the mind and heart, scores of little altars
are hurriedly erected to fill the empty space. Perhaps
all the holy places are just mounting evidences of the
truth that the real alternative to monotheism is not
atheism or agnosticism, but polytheism. When there
is no real High Altar of reverence, a lot of jerry-built
side-show altars spring up. They meet a need for ven-
eration. So probably every sport will have its shrine,
and every activity, including the Hardy Pioneers of
Needlework and the Twelve Apostles of Croquet.

If St. Paul were to look at our cities with the keen
eyes with which he looked at Athens, he would see
many shrines to many very minor gods, and he would
say, "Ye men (and women) of America, I perceive that
in every way you are very religious."

Perhaps these multiplying holy places point in the
direction of the central tragedy of the twentieth century. The words "hail" and "heil" come from the same
root. Perhaps it is true, as many have thought, that if
man does not say "Hail!" to an august God he is bound
to say "Heil!" to some little tin-pot deity.

Yours,

SIMEON STYLITES.

The Cultivation of Vanity

Sir: May I have the floor for a moment to speak a piece on behalf of a trait of human nature which is usually regarded as one of Satan's masterpieces? The wicked demon for which I have become attorney for the defense is Vanity.

Vanity has taken a pretty hard beating from the godly and the moralists through the years. Some people have even renounced the "vain glory of the world" in a baptismal covenant (a somewhat hasty step). The Bible is rough on vanity, particularly about not "lifting up the soul unto vanity." That bothered me quite a lot in my early days. There was no penalty attached in the 24th Psalm, but I feared the worst. I used to wonder what was in store for the little girls I saw at dances; they were certainly lifting up, if not their souls, at least their heads, unto vanity in the mirrors, poking their curls around to achieve a more potent magic. Vanity was definitely bad.

So it was an eye-opener to me when I came across a remark made by that amazing invalid Alice James, the sister of William and Henry. Alice was deeply depressed by reading the endless hypochondriac recordings of George Eliot in her published letters and journals, and finally bursts out in her journal:

What an abject coward she seems to have been about physical pain, as if it weren't degrading enough to have headaches, without jotting them down in a row to stare at one for all time, thereby defeating the beneficent law which provides that pain is forgotten. If she related her diseases and "depressions" and told for the good of others what armor she had forged against them, it would be conceivable, but they were simply cherished as a vehicle for a moan. Where was the creature's vanity?

There you have it — vanity a minister of grace! What kept Alice James on a higher level, so that she could refuse, as she said, to "accept the horizon of invalidism"? Many things, of course. But one force was vanity, the creation of a *persona* to which she lived up, too vain to sink down to making life the "vehicle of a moan."

A lawyer, very effective before court and jury, has written that he learned to speak by reason of vanity. Once in his early years he was addressing a large political meeting, and a perverse breeze blew from the stand his whole battery of notes and scattered them down into the audience. He had to decide in a split second whether to suffer the humiliation of having them picked up and restored or indulge the luxury of making a lordly gesture and saying gaily, "Don't bother, I don't need them!" He chose the gesture of vanity, took off into the air, made a safe landing, and lived happily ever after, free from notes.

It is incontestably true that a good supply of vanity helps to lift and keep a person up to the level of good manners — a good level on which to live, and a high one too. Many a person is too vain to raise a rumpus over an accident in a restaurant — being anointed with a sprinkling of soup, for instance. The reason may be that he is a truly noble character, but he had better give at least an "assist" to vanity, the necessity to keep up the pose of living on a higher level than that of a bad-tempered crab.

In many homes there is a little dressing table where the noble wife and mother can look into the mirror when she is applying lipstick and other bits of legerdemain. It is called a "vanity," a sound piece of furniture. Every home should have one. A man is out of luck when his wife becomes so saintly that she ceases to be a bit vain about her personal appearance. And vanity can be a spiritual force. There are many times when a new tricky little red hat will do more for a woman's spiritual morale than a dozen prayer meetings. Honest!

Yours,

SIMEON STYLITES.